Jews
Milk
Goats

Published by: The Gables Press

Paperback ISBN: 978-1-7384472-0-6
eBook ISBN: 978-1-7384472-1-3

Cover Design and Interior Layout by Spiffing Publishing.

Jews Milk Goats

Gill Freedman

For Jeremy, Seth and Rosa

CONTENTS

Preface

Chapter One
Bottle Feeding and Purim 11

Chapter Two
The Hippy Trail to Devon 16

Chapter Three
London and Lviv 24

Chapter Four
Off We Go Again 34

Chapter Five
A Festival of Freedom and Confinement 50

Chapter Six
Shavuot and Sheep Tails 54

Chapter Seven
Celebrations And Condolences 59

Chapter Eight
Feline Friends 67

Chapter Nine
The Buzz Of Summer 74

Chapter Ten
New Beginnings, Apples And Prayers 80

Chapter Eleven
Goats And Antisemitism 95

Chapter Twelve
Succot The Feast Of Tabernacles And The Birds 120

Chapter Thirteen
    To Remember The Past And Look To The Future 139

Chapter Fourteen
    Light In The Darkness 157

Acknowledgements 181

About The Author 183

PREFACE

As I finished writing Jews Milk Goats a horror story unfolded in the Middle East.

On October 7th, which coincided with the Sabbath and the Holy Day of Simchat Torah, 1,400 citizens of Israel were murdered in the most gruesome way.

Two hundred and fifty young people were gunned down at a music festival. Instead of dancing they found themselves running for their lives.

Kibbutzim close to the Gaza border were ransacked and burnt to the ground. Inside these agricultural settlements whole families were shot in cold blood – children in front of parents and parents in front of children. Babies were beheaded and civilians were tied up, raped and tortured and many of them burnt to cinders. 239 hostages ranging from nine month old babies to Holocaust survivors were taken as hostages and imprisoned in Gaza.

The videos of these vicious attacks were filmed by the killers who posted them on social media as they laughed, smoked cigarettes and gloried in their bloody rampage.

Rockets rained down on Israel from Gaza and bombs targeted the Hamas infrastructure in and around Gaza City. A blockade was put in place to prevent food, water and fuel from entering the Strip. Foreign nationals were prevented from leaving and, at time of writing, remain in limbo.

Over 1,000,000 civilians moved from Gaza city to the south. In Israel 100,000 people were internally displaced.

As I type I am living from hour to hour, listening to news on the radio, watching television reports at night and in between times distracting myself with the animals, the garden and the daily chores. I am blessed to have such distractions.

British Jews number less than 300,000 out of a population approaching 70,000,000. Every British Jew I know has friends or relatives in Israel and all of them have sons, sons-in-law, grandsons and husbands who have been called up to the army. They have left behind frightened grandparents, mothers, wives, sisters, children and babies. Many will not return alive and many will return with life-changing injuries.

In Gaza thousands of civilians have died and been injured. Families are running out of food and water, and many have lost their homes. By the time this book is printed there will be many more deaths and injuries of civilians and combatants.

I was born here as were both my parents and two of my grandparents. My other two grandparents immigrated to Britain as babies and this country was the only home they knew. My paternal grandfather signed up during the First World War and fought at the Battle of the Somme.

All four grandparents loved this country as did my parents, as do I.

Now, as I watch the war in the Middle East unfold and engulf the region, kill and maim and terrify so many innocents and possibly draw many other countries into a horrific conflagration, I wonder if my days here are numbered.

Read on........

CHAPTER ONE –
BOTTLE FEEDING AND PURIM

I threw my wig onto the back seat and put my foot down to cover the 50 miles home. I was anxious to get there before midnight and on a quiet road the journey would take less than an hour. Next to me Jeremy had closed his eyes and was in a deep, whisky sleep so I turned on the radio for company.

As we approached the gate I prodded my passenger. 'Come on, wake up. I need you to go inside and put the kettle on and I'll run upstairs and take these clothes off. The bottles are in the fridge. Please get them out as soon as we get indoors.'

I changed out of my party frock and into milk-spattered trousers and a hoodie. Jeremy was wide awake now and in the kitchen, warming the bottles by standing them in large cups of hot water. As I opened the back door he grabbed the torch and lit up a path as we strode into a field full of ewes and lambs to feed PJ and Ponyo. The twins' mother growled at us and stamped her foot. Poor old Mother Domino didn't understand that her scarred udder couldn't produce enough milk for her two-week-old boy and girl. It had been this way for the past three years since Domino developed mastitis and each season we had to help raise her lambs, much to her disgust.

It was Purim night and we had dressed up for the reading of the Megillah – The Book of Esther – in the synagogue in Borehamwood. The story of the beautiful virgin Esther, the Persian King Ahasuerus – Xerxes – and his antisemitic adviser Haman is an excuse for Jews around the world to celebrate their deliverance from genocide back in the year 650 BCE. To mark our survival we put on fancy dress, send each other gifts of chocolates, sweets, wine and cakes, give money to charity and drink until we can't tell the difference between the names of the hero and the villain of the story. What's not to like? We listen to the story on the night of the festival of Purim and then a second time the following morning. The theme of the narrative runs throughout our history, 'They tried to kill us, they failed, let's eat!'

Under the light of a watery moon and the beam from the torch, two hungry lambs bleated as they ran towards us, opened their mouths and glugged at their bottles of milk. In less than two minutes they were finished and had disappeared to find their mother and their friends.

We had time for less than five hours' sleep before the alarm woke us and at 5.30 am Jeremy drove the 50 miles back to Borehamwood to attend synagogue for the early morning reading of the Megillah. I had arranged to join him three hours later for a recital at the house of the rabbi for those of the community who wanted a more leisurely start to the day. That worked well for us. I would feed the lambs, open up the chicken houses and let the goats out into the paddock.

The best laid plans at The Gables don't always work out. It was 7.30 am and I was giving PJ and Ponyo their breakfast bottles when I heard a groaning noise coming from the other side of the barn. When the bottles were empty I went to investigate. Sitting on the straw, looking up to the roof and frothing at the mouth was Surprise, an 18 month old ewe who had never lambed before. Poking out of her backside was a head and it was stuck. Surprise was in pain and I was in a panic.

Two years before Jeremy and I had helped Pinky to deliver twins. The first emerged easily but Pinky was too tired to push out the second lamb. We were in trouble and called our neighbour, 'We need help, Kate, are you able to come over now?'

'I know about cows but I've never worked with sheep, but I'll be there,' she said, much to my relief. 'Shall I call Farmer Rob?'

'Yes please, but leave him a message. He doesn't usually answer his phone when he's working.'

Within a few minutes there were three of us trying to free the second lamb and I was Googling furiously and found out that we needed a tiny lamb lasso to tie around the baby's head and then, somehow pull the lamb through the birth canal. We thought we would lose both mother and lamb. Then in the nick of time the gate opened and Farmer Rob drove in, jumped out of his pickup truck, dressed in his trademark jeans and leather boots and joined us in the barn. He knelt down, tucked his long blonde hair behind his ears before he inserted the string into Pinky, placed the noose around the lamb's face and gently began to pull.

'I don't think that the lamb will survive but we have to get her out.' His concern showed on his furrowed brow as he continued the delicate manoeuvre. We were holding Pinky as Rob did his work and then, amazingly, a girl lamb emerged, alive and bleating. Some people are what we call horse whisperers who have a way of calming the animals down and taming them. Rob uses his whispering skills to speak to cows and sheep to make them feel safe.

But now on Purim morning I was in the barn on my own and there wasn't time to call Kate or Farmer Rob. Every minute was vital. Surprise might have been in labour all night. There was no way of knowing. I threw off my coat, rolled up the sleeves of my jumper and quite literally took matters into my own hands, grabbing Surprise's horns and shouting at her, 'Stand up girl. We have to work on this together.' As I wrapped my palms around the lamb's head and began to pull, the head and front legs started to emerge. 'Push, Surprise, we need one big push.' I don't know if Surprise understood me but a few seconds later the lamb slithered out covered in blood and mucus, floppy and lifeless. Poor little creature. She lay still on the straw as I cleared the veil of mucus from her nose and mouth. She gave a flutter. Alive? I rubbed her sides and belly and she twitched again. Lifting her gently I placed the lamb in front of her mother's nose. Surprise sniffed and put her muzzle near to the lamb which amazingly let out a tiny bleat. As I dipped my bloody hands into a bucket of water I suddenly felt cold and began to shake. I grabbed my coat, put it on and zipped it up to my chin and then I stood watching Surprise begin to lick the lamb clean. 'Good girl, Surprise, you have your first lamb and it's a girl.' I stroked her side and gave her a kiss on the top of her head. Surprise made mothering noises. Sheep really do speak if you listen. There are different sounds for different situations. A ewe and her lamb will call to each other across a field of noisy sheep, picking out their unique cries and finding one another, even in the dark. I didn't want to leave the barn, I just wanted to watch and savour the moment but I had to finish the morning chores, opening up the goat house, feeding chickens, ducks and geese and filling feeders and water containers. Just fifteen minutes later when I returned to check on Surprise the lamb was trying to stand and calling out loudly. She was beautiful and perfect. I reluctantly left mother and baby, went into the house, washed and changed into clean clothes and took a last peek in the barn before I drove back to London. Little Esther was on her feet and searching for her mother's teat. What a Purim miracle.

One hour later as I sat in the rabbi's house in London listening to the story of the deliverance of the Jews from wicked Haman's plans, I couldn't help smiling. I wondered how many of the nearly 300,000 thousand British Jews were leading such a schizophrenic existence. I didn't know of any other Jews who were living on farms or smallholdings. Certainly not religiously observant Jews. 'They should try it,' is what I thought. 'It's a great life. It can be done.'

Eleven years earlier, back in London where we lived in 2012, Jeremy was approaching 60 and getting increasingly restless with too many hours spent sitting in his office. One Friday night during dinner, he suddenly announced, 'I want to grow vegetables in the garden!' I laughed, 'You're a divorce lawyer and you haven't lifted a spade for 30 years. You're too old to start digging!' Mum gave me a look across the table as if to say he was mad. That just made him even more determined. Within a week he had bought himself a heavy duty fork, long handled hoe, trowel and a watering can and soon our suburban back garden was dug over and Jeremy had planted strawberries and grapes, beans and herbs and built a soft fruit cage.

'Please leave me enough room for my deck chair and umbrella.'

He left me a square of grass not much bigger than a rug.

As the summer progressed and the plants began to grow and the strawberries to fruit, friends asked if they could bring their children and grandchildren to see what was growing. Jeremy picked French beans and I cooked and served them to guests at our Friday night table. There were fresh salads too and blackcurrants and raspberries. We shared the surplus berries with a Polish neighbour who made several jars of delicious jam. Soon the editor of our synagogue magazine heard about Jeremy's new venture and approached me one Saturday morning after the service as we all congregated in the synagogue hall drinking wine and eating crisps and biscuits and cake.

'People have been talking about your garden and I wondered if you and Jeremy would allow me to write an article about what you're growing. It would be best if I could come and take some photographs.' Jeremy preferred to keep out of the limelight but I thought it would be fun and I called Hilary after the weekend.

'Yes. We'll be happy for you to come and take pictures and have a chat about the garden.'

An illustrated feature was published in the next edition and, as Jeremy suspected, he was asked all about it when he went to synagogue the following week. He wasn't pleased with me nor with all the attention.

As the garden filled up new ideas began to develop and take shape in our minds.

'What if…' mused Jeremy, 'What if we could somehow find a way to move out of London.'

This wasn't the first time we'd had such thoughts.

CHAPTER TWO –
THE HIPPY TRAIL TO DEVON

A year before our grandson was born Jeremy had seen an advert in the *Law Society Gazette* looking for a divorce lawyer to relocate to Jersey. We booked two nights at a seafront hotel and took a short flight from City Airport, hiring a car with which to explore the island.

Mum was puzzled, 'Why on earth do you want to visit Jersey in February?'

'We just fancy a break. Jeremy's been so busy we thought it would be fun to take a trip,' I lied.

'But it won't be warm then and the hotels aren't exactly glamorous.' Mum's idea of a weekend away was somewhere hot with art galleries, shops and museums to browse in and a luxurious hotel with an excellent restaurant and top-class food.

She was right. On our trip to Jersey it rained non-stop and the best hotel was an updated version of a boarding house. We drove around the island and realised that houses with land were outside of our budget and food shopping would be difficult as none of the shops stocked kosher food. The law practice on Jersey was keen to offer Jeremy a position but he wasn't sure that there would be enough work to keep him fully occupied and I didn't think that I would be happy. An even more pressing problem was that the tiny Jewish community numbered just 85 souls out of a total population of 108,000. We located the Jewish cemetery and even the headstone of the father of someone we knew in London. There was definitely no longer an active, vibrant and viable group of living Jews to make up the quorum of men needed to sustain Sabbath or festival services in the only synagogue on the island. It quickly became clear that Jersey was not for us.

Once the thought of moving had been planted our restlessness grew. As the fruit and vegetables took over our suburban garden we again began to make plans.

We were running out of space but not of ideas. We had form.

In 1978, three years after our marriage, we had swapped our small Victorian house in London for a run-down thatched cottage in Devon with two acres. Our heads were filled with hippy dreams of living off the land whilst Jeremy studied at Exeter University and I worked as a physiotherapist.

The Old Forge came with a few ramshackle outbuildings, a large untended garden and two not quite contiguous fields. The house nestled in a tiny hamlet at the foot of Stoneshill, two miles from the village of Sandford, three miles from the town of Crediton and ten miles from the City of Exeter. We were in our early 20s, money was tight and we drove old bangers that were barely roadworthy. What we lacked in ready cash we made up for in enthusiasm and energy. We were young and strong and we were prepared to work hard to realise our dreams.

'How are we going to know what to do?' I asked Jeremy on more than one occasion. Ever the optimist and visionary in our marriage he would say, 'We'll look it up, we'll ask the neighbours, we'll just learn as we go along.' And we did.

Inside the house the kitchen at the Old Forge was fitted with an ancient coal fired Rayburn range and once we got the knack of lighting it and adjusting the temperature we baked and cooked on it and in it. Each morning the first one up would riddle the Rayburn and put the ashes outside, stoke it up with coal and get it going. The kitchen was always warm and the range heated the water for the bathroom and the kitchen sink. Muffin, the tabby cat, sat on top of the Rayburn on cold winter days. Peggy, our collie cross spaniel, curled up in her basket beside the oven at night and we dried our laundry above it on a wooden dryer suspended from the ceiling. Once, when one of our sheep gave birth to a poorly lamb we tried to revive it by placing her inside the oven with the door open (we weren't trying to cook the lamb but we didn't know what else to do!). She didn't make it and we buried her in the garden. All the bedrooms were cold and in the depths of winter we often woke to find a thin layer of ice on the inside of the windows.

Two years after we moved to the cottage our son was born. He was a bonny 9lb 4oz baby who ate greedily and enjoyed lying in his pram in the garden watching the trees wave above him in the fresh Devon air. I breastfed him for several months and then he progressed from mother's milk to raw goats' milk and plenty of organic, home cooked and pureed fruit and vegetables. It was a great start in life and he was an exceptional sleeper from the age of ten weeks, going through the night and having two naps a day in the garden. We had no way of heating the baby's room and in the morning we would bring him down to the kitchen to bathe and then change and dress him on the wooden table. One day I turned around for a second and the baby, who had never moved before, rolled off the table and onto the hard floor. He and I were both in shock and then he let out a terrible cry. I picked him up, cuddled him tight, kissed him as I said, 'I'm so sorry, baby, I didn't know you could roll. I'm so sorry.' His crying turning to whimpering as I zipped up his all-in-one, bundled him into the car and drove straight to Crediton to see the Doctor. I felt terrible and probably cried more than the baby and it got worse when the Doctor said, 'You young women have no sense of responsibility. How could you possibly leave a baby on a table? You are very lucky that he seems to be unharmed except for that swollen lip.' I was mortified. From then on the changing mat went onto the floor.

There was a community of hippies around Devon. Some had stayed on after university, others had moved into communes or cheap rented accommodation in old farmhouses and cottages. We met up in local pubs or at each other's houses. One day Phil, who wasn't part of the hippy crowd but had hooked up with one of the hippy women we knew and liked, turned up at The Old Forge with a proposition. Phil was a bit of a wheeler dealer with a murky past and he was always looking for an opportunity to make some money.

'I've got a mate who has a herd of Jersey cows. He has three calves he wants to sell and I thought we could go halves. I'll help you get the shed fitted out with stalls and then we can put them in there and share looking after them.'

We took the plunge and Daisy, Bluebell and Clover came to live in the hastily partitioned stable. They had enormous lash-fringed eyes, dun-coloured coats that were silky to the touch and long, licky tongues.

A few months after we had moved to The Old Forge we arrived home from Exeter one afternoon to find a young woman sitting in our kitchen. Nobody we knew ever locked their door in Devon unless they were going away on holiday. I often popped in to see friends and would sit in their living room until they returned from shopping or just used their house as a convenient place to feed the baby and make myself a cuppa before leaving them a note and going on my way. 'Hello,' said the stranger, 'I'm Barbara and I live in the house at the top of Stoneshill. I thought it was about time that I came and introduced myself. You'll see me drive past every day on the way to and from the dairy.' We were a bit surprised at Barbara's chutzpah and I wasn't sure that either of us would have let ourselves into her kitchen on a first meeting, but Barbara was an eccentric and unusual 22 year old. She worked for a local farmer as a dairy maid and managed her own small herd of milking goats. Over the course of the next few weeks and over many pots of tea Barbara worked on her plan to persuade us to buy our own goats. Jeremy did his research and decided that we would try our hand at goat keeping. My grandma had given me some money for my birthday and that was just enough for the purchase of the animals. Barbara was delighted. She located two white Saanens that were for sale and very quickly the price was agreed with the owners and the goats were delivered to The Old Forge. I spoke with grandma Anne on the telephone and discussed names. Grandma liked Penelope and I was keen on Prudence and that is what we called the girls. That same afternoon Barbara called in on her way to work.

'You haven't come to see us,' I laughed. 'You're really here to get a look at the new arrivals. Come on I'll take you to see them.' She grinned and took a piece of straw out of her unruly red hair. Barbara always smelled of animals, wore farmer's overalls and held fierce opinions. She, Jeremy and I would sit around the farmhouse table drinking mugs of tea and eating warm rock buns straight from the Rayburn and Barbara would rant on about, 'Communists and students who don't know how to do a day's work. Hippies are just a bunch of layabouts.' Barbara and I enjoyed a good ding dong and although we often had our differences we would laugh as much as we shouted at each other. She was a good friend. When Barbara was away we would milk her goats and she looked after ours when we went to London to see our family. It was a great arrangement. Her loud voice and tough veneer hid a heart of gold and she regularly left presents for us outside our front door – a pint of creamy gold top milk for Jeremy and a basket of field mushrooms or a giant puffball for me.

Jeremy and I, accompanied by Muffin the cat and Peggy the dog, went on long walks starting up Jack Backs Lane at the side of our house, and across the hedge-fringed fields where we picked blackberries, sloes, rosehips and elderberries and harvested wild mushrooms. All this was food for free and it gave us a thrill to make a huge pot of soup, a bottle of sloe gin, blackberry jam, elderberry wine and rosehip syrup from these plentiful gifts of nature. Our bibles were a book by John Seymour called 'Self Sufficiency' and an American Encyclopaedia by some backwoods survivalists that gave advice on everything from pickling vegetables to natural childbirth and killing ducks and geese. Dubious advice for the two of us who were and remain committed vegetarians.

We quickly got to know our neighbours and formed friendships which continued even when we later sold up and relocated to London. A renowned potter and sculptor, John Maltby and his wonderfully kind and intelligent wife Heather lived a few yards down the road in a house that they had designed themselves to accommodate a studio and a small showroom. Whenever mum visited The Old Forge we would pop over to the Maltbys and buy seconds. Mum and I thought that these pieces were sold cheaply because of some artistic flaw that only John could see. To us they were perfect works of art. John and Heather's teenage daughter, Phillipa became our go-to babysitter when our son was born and her brother, Joe, often crossed the quiet road to play a game of chess with Jeremy. We were friends with the whole family and we were as close in age to the teenage children as to their parents. 11 years later, when we had moved back to London, we invited them all to our son's barmitzvah party when he turned 13, marking his entry into Jewish manhood with its religious obligations. We were thrilled that they joined us and John made our son a unique chess set which he treasures to this day.

Next door to us was a two up, two down thatched cottage which was occupied by a young social worker who had moved out to the hamlet when her husband died. I felt so sorry for her and wondered if moving to such an isolated spot was a good idea. We were friendly but she seemed to want to spend evenings and weekends on her own. After a month or two of this isolation she asked us if we knew where she could find a kitten to adopt. A friend of ours had a cat who had just given birth to a litter and we arranged to take her to see them. She picked out a fluffy, white kitty which came to live in the cottage and kept her company. A few weeks later she knocked on our door and offered to help feed our chickens in return for some of the eggs. The arrangement lasted for about six months and then, happily, she met a new man and she and the kitten moved away and we lost touch. The little cottage was then sold to a pair of retired women who appeared quite prim and proper until we got to know them better and discovered that they were feisty and fun. They got me extremely drunk one night when we joined them for a drink in their house. Frieda, the elder of the two, had strong opinions and was definitely authoritarian, old fashioned and conservative in the extreme and she disapproved of abbreviated names. 'If your name is Gillian then that is what I will call you, not Gill, and Jeremy is definitely not Jerry!' She also poured extremely large whiskies into cut glass crystal tumblers. The two of them moved on to warmer climes within a couple of years and went to live in Spain where they enjoyed the sun, sangria and sea. Years after we had all left Devon Frieda would write me a Christmas card in her beautiful copperplate handwriting written in black ink with a proper fountain pen. I remain in touch with her partner even though Frieda died some years ago.

The couple directly opposite our cottage were friendly to us and the wife, an NCT – National Childbirth Trust – breastfeeding counsellor, often brought their four beautiful children over to our yard to visit and play with the goats and cows and chickens. The husband was a busy solicitor, slightly pompous in his manner and not as friendly to us as his wife. Maybe he thought that these two long-haired hippies would lower the tone of the hamlet or perhaps he was envious of our lifestyle. Possibly he was just unhappy. He was supposed to be in charge of their unruly black Labrador, Pepper, who the local farmer, Peter Isaacs accused of killing one of his sheep. The Isaacs' farm was half way up the hill and he and his sons raised animals as well as hiring themselves out for contract work on other farms. Farmers guard their livestock fiercely for several reasons. Each healthy animal represents part of the income of the farm and any loss affects the balance sheet. There is a close bond between farmers and the stock that they raise, especially on a small acreage where the farmer will recognize each creature and even have favourites with pet names. Pepper's owner adamantly denied responsibility for the dead sheep. 'It's definitely nothing to do with our dog,' he told Farmer Isaacs.

'What do you call this?' the farmer shouted when he found bones and guts in the courtyard of our neighbour's house after an unpleasant and noisy confrontation that we could hear across the road in our cottage. It was obvious that the Labrador was guilty.

'I'll shoot that dog if he ever comes near my sheep again.' It was no idle threat.

We didn't talk about being Jewish back in our Devon days. The town of Crediton, the village of Sandford and our hamlet, Stoneshill, were almost exclusively white English and there was just one black guy who lived in the town. He, unlike us, couldn't hide his identity even if he had wanted to because the colour of his skin marked him out as different. Devon in the 1970s was insular, ethnically white and religiously Christian and outsiders who had relocated to the county were derided as grockles. We were not only grockles from London but Jewish too. Although we could pass as white and we were English I always wished that I could have been braver and talked about my Jewish identity and background. In those days antisemitism and racism were not only tolerated, they were rife and infected every area of life, as I will explain later. I would have liked to speak about our visits to London to join our families for the Jewish High Days and Holy Days but we decided to keep quiet.

Exeter has a tiny synagogue built in 1764. It is the third oldest active synagogue in the country after Bevis Marks in the City of London and the synagogue in Plymouth. The community, never very large, had almost disappeared by the 20th century but it was revived by some local enthusiasts in 1980 and we attended the reopening ceremony. There we discovered Jews from as far afield as Somerset, Dorset and Cornwall, all eager to connect with each other. I talked with one girl who was dressed in jeans tucked into muddy wellington boots and was cradling a baby in her arms.

'Where have you come from?'

'We've driven all the way from just outside Looe to get here.'

'That's one helluva journey. It must have taken ages.'

The girl sighed. 'I promised my mum we would come. She read about the synagogue in the Jewish Chronicle and she's been nagging me ever since. Mum couldn't believe that there were other Jews like us out here. We do love it in our village but we haven't actually told anyone that we're Jewish.'

I understood her reticence. It was a lovely afternoon meeting Jews from across the South West of England but as we all lived so far from each other we were unlikely to get together except for special occasions at the synagogue.

This nearly carefree, idyllic lifestyle in Devon continued for less than five years and then we reluctantly returned to London when I was pregnant with our second child.

CHAPTER THREE –
LONDON AND LVIV

It was time to join the 'rat race' as we called it. Jeremy qualified as a lawyer, opened his own practice and we stayed put in the city for the next 30 years. Mum and dad were delighted we were home.

'We hated coming to visit you in Devon,' Mum confessed. 'It was always cold in the bedroom and it was so muddy outside. Dad really didn't want to miss his golf and his bridge but we did it because we wanted to see our grandson. Thank goodness you've come back.'

London had its advantages. The local state schools were excellent and close by and the children could visit shows and concerts and join chess and sports clubs. Stumps, the cricket team Jeremy and his friend Ray had started when they graduated, was still going strong and Jeremy returned to his position as wicket keeper.

'Jerry, good to have you back. Nobody else really wanted to keep wicket,' admitted Ray. It's a dangerous position and not kind on the finger joints, but Jeremy loved it. The North London cricket grounds weren't as pretty as those in Devon but I was more than happy to go along to watch the team and keep an eye on the young children who played together on the boundary. All the youngsters were treated to squash and crisps in pub gardens at the end of the afternoon and these were happy times spent in the fresh air with friends and their families.

Cricket was a very different affair when we lived in Devon. In Sandford village when Jeremy asked to join the local cricket club he was told by the captain in no uncertain terms, 'We have a rule here. Your wife will have to make tea twice a season or you can't play. We expect homemade scones, jam and cream and cucumber and egg sandwiches.' Women's lib had yet to reach rural Devon and the only wife who was exempt from tea duties was the Captain's missus who kept the scorebook. In liberated

London our multicultural, feminist cricket team, 'Stumps', had a different rule. 'If you want to play,' Jeremy would tell new recruits, 'Then you, not your wife or girlfriend, have to make a tea of sandwiches and biscuits at least once a season. Nothing fancy.'

My sport was tennis. Several clubs were near to our home and all of them would have been pleased to accept new members and so I joined Templars Tennis Club and became a member of the team which competed in a North London midweek women's league.

I thought back to my childhood tennis lessons in the 1960s when prejudice against Jews, Afro-Caribbeans and Asians was tolerated and socially acceptable in English society. There was a club, the prestigious Cumberland Lawn Tennis and Squash Club, close to where we lived and I asked Mum, 'Why can't Michael and I have our tennis lessons there?' Instead, we had to take a much longer bus ride and then walk to take part in a group lesson in Golders Green. Mum just said, 'The Cumberland doesn't let Jews play there.' I later found out that the Wimbledon Doubles Champion, Angela Buxton, had faced the same ban from The Cumberland several years earlier. She lived around the corner from the club and had been sent by her school to take lessons with the coach. When she repeatedly asked about club membership the teacher told her, 'Look, Angela, please don't keep asking me, you're not going to be able to join the club because you're Jewish.'

Angela Buxton later partnered with the black American tennis player, Althea Gibson, who had been similarly mistreated at competitions and clubs in America because of the colour of her skin. The two outcasts went on to win the Ladies Doubles Title at the French Championships and then Wimbledon in 1956. In spite of their victories both continued to face exclusion and racism and Angela Buxton eventually set up her own small tennis club near to where Jeremy and I and our children lived in North London.

My parents came up against the same barriers when they wanted to play golf. The nearby Hampstead and Highgate golf clubs had Jewish quotas. Mum and dad certainly didn't want to play at a club which didn't want them so they joined one of the many Jewish golf clubs that had been set up to cater for them and their friends. They drove all the way from St Johns Wood to Potters Bar for their sport but at least they felt comfortable and could be themselves without trying to fit into a place where they knew that they were not welcome.

All the private and prestigious public schools had Jewish quotas too, usually limited to ten percent of the yearly intake of pupils. It shocks me today to realise that we all knew about these barriers, accepted them, kept our heads down and didn't want to 'make a fuss.' Like minorities everywhere we knew that we just had to try harder to succeed and even then we might never truly be accepted.

On Friday nights, when we had left Devon and were living in London once again, we hosted Sabbath evening dinners for family and friends and occasional strangers or, as my children called them, 'the waifs and strays.' The Jewish tradition encourages Hachnasos Orchim – welcoming and giving hospitality to guests – and we were pleased to invite people of all ages especially those who were widowed or living alone in London without family. I once sat next to a lone Israeli tourist at the theatre, we got talking and then she joined us the same week for a traditional Friday night meal. Hospitality ensures anyone who wants a meal is included and no one is left on their own week after week. This is one of my favourite customs and I hope if I am ever by myself or in a strange land I will be able to count on the hospitality of other Jews. On Sabbath mornings Jeremy and I and the children attended the local orthodox synagogue. Jeremy became a regular participant in the services where he sat downstairs with the men and I sat upstairs in the ladies' gallery with our daughter reading from our prayer books and observing the proceedings below. Afterwards, when the service concluded, all of us, men, women and children would meet up in the adjoining hall to eat and drink, mingle and chat with each other and our friends. As a family we were comfortable with these rules of separation in the prayer hall, although some of our friends felt happier in a less traditional synagogue setting where men and women sat together and participated equally in the service. Friday nights and Sabbaths shaped our week and gave us 25 hours away from the constant demands of the office.

On the Sabbath the rules, which may seem strict to outsiders, feel liberating to those who keep them. Observant Jews don't use their telephones or tech or watch television on the Sabbath. They don't go shopping, wash clothes, use cars or do any form of everyday work from one hour before sunset on Friday until three stars are seen in the Saturday night sky. These constraints gift us time to spend with the children, to play games with them, to read books and newspapers and eat leisurely meals and socialise. As the children grew older there was a youth service in the synagogue as well as clubs and a lively social scene. My mother-in-law used to say, quoting the secular Jewish writer Asher Ginsberg who was known as the founder of cultural Zionism, 'It's not the Jews who kept the Sabbath but the Sabbath that kept the Jews.'

Jews are obliged by the Torah to look out for each other, to lend money to the poor, to care for widows and orphans, to visit and care for the sick and even to redeem hostages. Tzedakah, which is loosely translated as charity, is a fundamental tenet of observant Jewish life and extends not only to fellow Jews but beyond into the wider non-Jewish world. It was hardly surprising that the rabbi of our synagogue agreed at the annual conference of European Rabbis in 1992 to twin our prosperous community in North London with the emerging Jewish community in Lviv, a major city of the newly independent Ukraine. When the Soviet Union collapsed in 1991 the gate was opened for Jewish organizations to send their shelichim – messengers – to countries, cities and towns where Jewish practice, knowledge and worship had almost been extinguished first by the Nazis and then by Communism. The synagogue board members agreed to add a small, voluntary levy to our annual synagogue bills. This money was sent to the young American Rabbi, Mordechai Bald and his new bride, Sara as they struggled to feed, clothe, educate and care for the emerging Jews who had hidden their identity for so many years.

Lviv lies in a strategically important position close to the Polish border. Under Austro-Hungarian rule it was known as Lemberg, under Polish rule Lwow, following its liberation from the Nazis by Russia it was called Lvov and since independence it has been called Lviv. Before the 2nd World War a third of the city's 300,000 inhabitants was Jewish. After the Holocaust just a handful of Jews had survived by living in the sewers beneath the street.

The Soviets moved people around their empire and other Jews were relocated to the city after its liberation. It was thought that when we twinned our two communities 4,000 citizens identified as Jews.

In 1997 Rabbi Jackson, approaching retirement, decided that he would organize a group to travel to Lvov (as we still called it) to see how our money was being spent and what more might be required. I took no notice of the initiative but Jeremy was keen to join the trip. He had an ulterior motive. The itinerary included an overnight stop in Warsaw, just 50 km from his ancestral shtetl – village – of Gombin. Whilst the proposed group would make a tour of the capital of Poland he thought that he could take a taxi west from Warsaw to see the place where his great grandparents lived and about which he had heard all his life. I was not impressed with the idea of this trip to Poland and Ukraine but Rabbi Jackson was very persuasive. He had decided that our synagogue needed to visit our twin community in Lvov and he was not going to fail. He exerted all his Irish charm and pulled in a number of favours to persuade his mostly retired friends to sign up for the trip. The month was February, the cost was high and the ultimate destination, Lvov, a big unknown. Jeremy and I were the youngest participants by at least 20 years. The rest of the group was used to five-star hotels and business class travel. We were all in for a shock. Warsaw was bleak but Lvov was worse. The Soviet style hotel rooms had no soap, no towels or toilet paper (fortunately most of us had been warned) and the sheets were wringing wet from damp.

We were relieved to be met in the foyer by young Rabbi Mordechai and Sara, his Rebbetzin, who escorted us to the one functioning synagogue for a heimishe – home style – kosher meal in the synagogue dining room. This amazing young couple had been sent to the city from New York and on arrival they scarcely spoke a word of Russian or Ukrainian. They were living in a three room apartment with an intermittent water supply, no access to any home comforts and tasked with raising the money to run a school and educate and nurture a broken and fragile community. Most of the synagogue members lived in decrepit Soviet built blocks of flats on the outskirts of the city. Sara took us to meet some of the families in these homes. The lifts didn't work and the buildings were in dire need of repair. Those who lived in the city centre were in 19th century apartment buildings that looked beautiful from the outside but there was no lighting in the stairwells and few if any of the apartments had a bathroom. All the appliances in the kitchen were old and if there was a refrigerator we were shocked to see that there was hardly any food inside it or in the cupboards. The people in Lvov, Jews and non-Jews alike, were living a hand to mouth existence in a grim post-Soviet world. On the streets, in the hotel, in the markets it was rare to see smiling faces or to hear laughter. On one corner near the dusty and run down museum, an old man sat on the cold pavement. His wooden crutches were at his side and one leg was missing. Several army medals were attached to his old grey coat and he stretched out his hand to us. It was heartbreaking and I was heartbroken.

Later we travelled a mile or so out of the city to the notorious Janowska Road death Camp which was a forced labour camp set up by the Nazis in 1941 for mainly Jewish inmates who had to survive a 'selection' to decide if they were fit to work. Those who did not pass the test were sent on to Belzec for immediate extermination. Those in Janowska rarely lived for more than three months, starving on a pitiful diet, broken by hard labour and at the mercy of sadistic guards who shot at them for target practice. One who did miraculously escape was the famous Nazi hunter, Simon Weisenthal. Over 40,000 other Jews died in Janowska. Our group stood outside the gates of the camps, which the Soviets had mostly pulled down after the war and rebuilt as a prison. It was chilling to see and hear the barking of Alsatian dogs and to know that inside the wire fencing prisoners were living in such a terrible place. We bowed our heads, recited memorial prayers for the dead and then stood in silence as we contemplated the terrible fate and death so many of our brethren.

Sara and the Rabbi then took us to visit the Jewish school and kindergarten which were housed in dilapidated buildings with one farshtunken toilet at the back of some low-rise blocks of flats. In spite of the poor facilities the children were smiling and laughing and so happy to greet us, their rare foreign visitors. We were amazed at the performances of the children who welcomed us with a song in English and then recited and sang in Hebrew. All of us cried at their charm and beauty and then we cried as we watched a small, blind girl being held tightly by her teacher's hand so that she, too, could join in with the songs and dances. We were humbled beyond words. At supper that night we sat with the older men and women of the community in the synagogue dining room. Their clothes were worn and unfashionable, their teeth were bad, their faces were lined but their smiles and their pleasure at our visit overcame all the barriers of language. We once again felt humbled by their situation and the warmth of their welcome to us, visitors from a privileged western world. Shabbat in Lvov was special as we sat and prayed with the congregants, young and old in the synagogue where the walls and ceiling were painted with biblical scenes and mythical animals. Sara showed us the holes up high where, for sport, German officers had shot at some of the painted animals. It was a miracle that this synagogue had survived at all. Most in the city had not. The prayers were the same in London and Lvov. Just as we did back home in London, we lit two candles to usher in the Sabbath and we made a blessing over the chollah – the plaited bread Sabbath bread. The food was plain but wholesome and Sara had made a dish that I had only ever eaten before with my paternal grandmother. Kasha, or buckwheat, is a staple food in Ukraine and considered peasant food, but my brother and I loved it and used to beg our grandma Katy to make it for us. Grandma and her family had come to England from Odessa and I then realised that the dish I thought was so exotic and delicious was one that she would have eaten regularly as a child.

At the end of our trip it didn't take much for our rabbi to persuade me to take over the twinning of our two communities. His friends were, frankly, too old and had given many years of their lives to other charitable initiatives. It was down to me and to Jeremy to take the venture forward and we did so, beginning with another trip the following year when we press-ganged some younger travellers to join us and get involved with fund raising. There followed 20 years where I went to sleep every day thinking about Lvov and woke up with fresh ideas, typing letters on my home computer before going off to work. Our fundraising with the Lvov community became so time consuming that one day our teenage son announced that he was 'going to start a charity for children who are neglected ......by parents who run charities!' Happily both of our teenagers survived this benign neglect.

As time went on Ukranians wanted to emphasise their independence from Russia and they celebrated their national identity and culture. We learnt to use the Ukrainian name for the city, Lviv instead of the Russian name, Lvov. Our fundraising remained an integral part of the day to day budget for our twin community. A Cantorial concert was the vehicle used to promote and support Lviv and I, who had never appreciated cantorial singing in synagogue, became a sort of musical impresario – booking performers from around the world and persuading them to come to London to sing for over 600 people. I still wonder how we did it but when I thought of the Rabbi and his exceptional wife, living so far from home with such an immense job to do, I knew my work was easy by comparison. Then Jeremy, a man with vision and ideas a-plenty, decided that we had to help restore Lviv's one functioning synagogue to its former pre-war glory. A North London man, who was a well-known fundraiser, suggested that Jeremy cut his long hair to raise the seed money for the project. He guaranteed to get at least £20,000 for the haircut. Some friends opened their garden for the event and more money was pledged as Jeremy's locks fell to the ground. This was just the start. I would have to raise the rest and Jeremy wasn't taking 'no' for an answer. I knew that he was right. We had to prevent the building from falling into further disrepair and to save the magnificent artwork on the walls.

In Israel, that year, Jeremy and I went to see the Rebbe – the spiritual leader – of the Chassidic Stolin Karlin movement who had sent Rabbi Mordechai and Rebbetzin Sara to Lviv. We needed a blessing to be successful in our fundraising. He told us that we didn't need one and that the money was already there. A week or so after returning from Israel I turned on my computer and an email that I had sent out on spec to a philanthropist in New York had received a reply. He would fund the project which Jeremy and I would have to organise and supervise from start to finish. The project was on and we were fully committed. There was no going back.

Two years later, in 2007, we chartered a plane from Luton airport and 150 adults and children flew to Ukraine for a day trip that started at 4 am and finished after midnight. On that exceptional day we moved from darkness to light – from Janowska Road, through the streets of the old Jewish quarter, to the vibrant new Jewish School building funded by the Lauder foundation, to the market square and the beautiful Lviv opera house and onto the synagogue, where the Polish-style painted walls and ceiling had been painstakingly restored by the same art experts who had also worked on the restoration of Lviv's Cathedrals. We had insisted that the bullet holes remained in the ceiling so that no one should ever forget the cruelty and barbarity of the Nazis. Inside the synagogue hundreds of men, women and children gathered to welcome us, dance with us, sing with us and rejoice with us. The tables around the sides of the synagogue were laid out with dishes of food and we added bags of kosher sweets and biscuits we had brought with us from London, treats unavailable in Lviv. The Lviv children were thrilled and their parents and the old people were also excited at the array of delicacies on offer. One of our young people was upset when she told us that she had seen an old lady putting food into her bag. The reality was that life remained difficult for the old and infirm whose pensions did not cover their living expenses. Many of us were aware that but for the foresight and courage of our grandparents who, like so many poor and persecuted refugees then and now left their homes to seek a better life, we might be the ones relying on the charity of others.

That day was and remains one of the most memorable days of my life. Even though my fundraising ended when I left London and moved to Bedfordshire, my friendship with Rebbetzin Sara is enduring and unbroken. We message each other regularly, we care about each other's families and my admiration and love for Sara and her husband is boundless.

As I sit in The Gables in 2023, I am fearful that this synagogue, a remnant of a once vibrant Jewish community, might succumb to the fighting which is ravaging and destroying so much of present day Ukraine and killing and injuring so many human beings. It is a country that has seen so much tragedy over the centuries and its rich, black soil is too often soaked with blood. I think of Lviv and Ukraine every day.

My great grandparents left Ukraine in 1900 and as a result of their migration, three generations on we found ourselves living in Hampstead Garden Suburb, London. This leafy, green suburb was the embodiment of the vision of the Victorian social activist and campaigner Dame Henrietta and her husband Canon Samuel Barnett who she married in 1873. With the help of the renowned architects Sir Edwin Lutyens and Raymond Unwin, they designed a garden city next to Hampstead Heath with a variety and range of beautiful cottages and houses, a Quaker meeting house, churches, tea rooms, nursery school and sheltered housing for the elderly. Later a girls' grammar school and educational institute were established and named The Henrietta Barnett school in honour of the woman who had purchased the land and shaped its future. Henrietta and her husband hoped to see all classes living together in a light and airy environment. By the time we had moved to the Suburb the area had become an almost exclusively middle and upper middle-class enclave and a magnet for many Jewish families who were attracted by the Hampstead Garden Suburb Synagogue built in 1935 and enlarged in 1939 to accommodate the growing membership. There were shops within a minute's walk of our home which included a kosher restaurant, grocery and kosher bakery. Sometimes, on a Friday morning when I walked to the baker to buy the chollahs over which we would make a blessing at the Friday night dinner table, I could stop four or five times to chat with Jewish neighbours and friends. This was, in some ways delightful and comfortable, but in other ways it felt claustrophobic. It was our own privileged ghetto, a sheltered bubble far away from the reality of the secular world. Many of the Jewish children in our suburb went to the Jewish nursery and then primary school attached to the Synagogue. They graduated to one of three Jewish secondary schools or some of the private schools a coach ride away from home. Very few of these children ever went on a bus or underground tube and they rarely mixed with anyone outside of their Jewish social sets. This cosy isolation troubled me but, as a parent, I could see why their families wanted to protect their offspring from some of the more toxic and violent elements their children might have met in the big wide world. These kids were definitely not streetwise.

Once our own children had married and left home we could see the years stretching out comfortably in front of us but Jeremy and I were restless after more than thirty years in London. We wanted a fresh challenge. It was time for a change.

CHAPTER FOUR –
OFF WE GO AGAIN

In my parents' flat one Monday evening I told Mum and Dad about our plans to move out of London. I felt as though I was asking for their permission and they didn't initially voice any objections. But three days later Mum phoned me at work. She and Dad were worried. 'How are you going to manage in the countryside? There won't be any shops selling kosher food. There aren't any kosher restaurants. Where will you go to shul? What happens when one of us dies or Jeremy's parents? We're not getting any younger.'

These were questions we had already asked ourselves. When we started to think, talk and then plan our move to the countryside my very first question to Jeremy had been, 'What will do if one of our parents gets really ill?' Both of us had siblings and that allowed us to share any future caring responsibilities with our brothers. When a parent passes away sons are obliged to say mourning prayers every day for a year but this requirement is fulfilled even if only one brother is able to attend the synagogue. Jeremy had two brothers so between the three of them they could share this obligation and I, as a woman, was not obliged to say the memorial prayers at all. It looked as though aged parents would not stop our plans. We could buy kosher cheese and groceries in London, only 50 miles down the A1. Meat, which has to be ritually killed to be kosher and only allows the eating of animals that chew the cud and have cloven hooves, wasn't an issue because we had been vegetarians for all our married life. So that dealt with food. I wasn't a fan of eating out because kosher restaurants are usually extremely busy and noisy places. It seems to me that Jewish people speak more loudly than the English and are more inclined to stop and chat. In kosher restaurants we would frequently run into people we knew and by the time we had finished talking to them our food would be cold. I remember parents' evening at our son's Jewish secondary school. The chatter of the families in the main hall was almost deafening until the headmistress rang a bell and called out, 'Quiet please. Go outside if you want to talk.' In marked contrast we were struck by the subdued hum of polite conversation when we attended our daughter's secular grammar school to meet her teachers.

Our grandson voiced his opposition to our plans. 'I don't want you to move Grandma,' he complained, 'I like this place.' We and our house were inextricably linked in his four-year-old mind. I assured him that we would soon have a huge garden for football and all his toys would move with us to a bedroom in a new house. He remained sceptical. Our Jewish friends constantly asked us, 'How are you going to be Jewish when there's no shul nearby?' The main centres for Jewish life are in either London or Manchester and there wouldn't be a synagogue within walking distance of our country home. Observant Jews don't drive on the Sabbath and they couldn't understand how we, who had been so involved in communal and religious life, would cope with the isolation. Neither of us was worried. It would work itself out as we went along. Our non-Jewish and less religious and secular friends didn't give our move a second thought, they were excited and so were we.

The sale board went up outside our house. We had taken the first step and within two weeks we had a buyer. Then we contacted estate agents and made an offer on a thatched, Grade II listed house in Much Hadham but we were outbid. Our search resumed a few miles further up the A1 where prices were lower. One warm June day we set off to see three houses all within our budget and with five acres of land apiece. Two didn't sound promising. One, the Old Post Office, was in the centre of Wilden village overlooked on all sides. The other had been empty for ages. The surrounding fields were flat and dull and the outbuildings downright ugly. Even before we arrived at the last place I had a good feeling about The Gables. The house was set back from the road behind a high hedge making it invisible to passing cars. The village was half a mile away and like the Old Forge, there was one neighbour opposite and two more just along the road. Jeffrey, the jovial, Welsh owner met us with a smile and showed us the untended five acres which he called, 'My nature reserve. Which is just my excuse for not being bothered to cut the grass or dig the garden. I've got a ride-on mower so I cut a path for you but the grass is so high you can't see far.' At the far end of the garden was a natural pond surrounded by ash trees and a thicket of overgrown blackthorn and hawthorn hedge. Like everything at The Gables, in the summer sunshine it looked romantic in spite of its neglected and wild state. Jeffrey then took us to view the 300-year-old barn and the stable block, all of which were uninhabitable and unsafe. 'The building needs quite a lot of work,' he said turning to Jeremy. That was something of an understatement. The barn had a dirt floor and was open to the ravages of the elements. Jeremy looked up at the corrugated iron roof and opened his mouth in shock and amazement at the poor state of the building. 'We would have to let the barn fall down,' I whispered to Jeremy as we looked around the place, 'We can't afford to do it up as well as the house and the fields.' Jeffrey pretended not to hear my remarks. Jeremy said nothing but he was harbouring different ideas. I have learnt to worry when Jeremy falls silent. It usually means that he is hatching a plan and, of course, he was. Perhaps if I had known what we were stepping into I would have been less keen to take on the project but on the day that we saw The Gables the sun was shining, some roses were flowering and I fell in love with the place, hook, line and sinker. I never wanted to leave.

The Gables had been on and off the market for 18 months. The price had dropped to well below our budget, leaving us with money to spend on the renovations. Jeffrey, the vendor, was a solicitor who wanted to retire and move away. He cheekily asked, 'Jeremy, would you like to buy my practice as well as the house? The office is in the market square in St Neots and you can get there in twelve minutes if you're in a hurry.' Jeremy declined. We wanted a home not a business. Contracts were exchanged and signed in July and from the end of August we spent the next six months camping out at The Gables for half the week and the other half working in our office in London. We had to carry on earning a living while at the same time trying to tame the huge garden in Bedfordshire, organise fencing and a polytunnel and find a local builder to start on the work inside and outside the house. It was uncomfortable sleeping on the floor at The Gables and we appreciated the luxury of a real bed in a flat in town whilst we commuted. We were constantly tired, living on a diet of cheese sandwiches, crisps, apples and bananas and we had a deadline to move in fully by Christmas 2013.

The plan was to open our new home to friends and family so that we could celebrate festivals and occasional Sabbaths on the smallholding. We weren't trying to escape and become hermits.

There is no mains drainage in that part of the countryside and we needed to install a large septic tank to filter the waste and water of up to 30 people at a time. 'You don't need such a big piece of kit,' complained the builder that we had hired, 'There are only two of you.'

'We're expecting quite a few visitors,' I told him but he couldn't get his head around our plans and continued to think that we were crazy Londoners who didn't know what we were doing. He and the contractors carried out our orders nonetheless.

There was also a boiler and oil storage tank to fit and a new kitchen to replace the old and broken wooden units that we had inherited. The summer house was in dire need of roof repairs and we wanted to turn the huge, triple garage into three self-contained bedrooms and bathrooms so that family and friends could come and stay. There was a long and ever-lengthening list of improvements but we needed to set some limits and the aim was to get into the house and begin really 'living' at The Gables and not just visiting. Until the new heating system was in place we would fire up the large wood burner in the lounge and, one day decided to test the open fire in the small living room to make sure that we would be warm during the winter. Jeffrey's wife had left decorative pine cones in that fireplace and we soon discovered why. When we removed the ornaments and got the fire going the whole downstairs filled with smoke and we and the house smelled like burnt toast for days on end. We would in time purchase another wood burner.

On late summer evenings, after a long day working outside, we cracked open cold beers and sat on the swing seat at the back of the house. Looking out over the paddock there was a large oak tree standing proud beyond the perimeter of the field. At twilight the branches filled with roosting crows bedding down for the night high above the hedges. The huge skies were tinged with blue, pink, purple and shades of red at sunset and we watched the changing vista day after day and marvelled at the colours. 'We never really noticed the sky in London,' I remarked to Jeremy.

'It was always there,' he said, 'But the buildings got in the way.' Our predecessor had mentioned that there was a barn owl at The Gables and one evening we were thrilled by the sight of a white bird flying low over the paddock and resting on a fence post. An owl is such an extraordinary creature and I had never before seen one in the wild. The barn owl has a short body, a large heart-shaped head and powerful, wide wings that beat gracefully as the bird glides over the fields searching for small mammals on which to prey. Occasionally I catch sight of an owl as I drive home in the dark or glimpse one sitting on a branch in the ash tree next to the front gate and every time I can almost feel my heart skip a beat. Once I woke in the night and saw a ghostly white form flying past our bedroom window. It sent shivers down my spine.

That evening on the back porch I turned to Jeremy and said, 'That's just awesome. I feel so privileged to be sitting here and watching an owl flying across our field.'. I looked over at my husband and smiled. His hair, like mine, was still long and worn in a pony tail. No longer dark brown his fine hair was streaked with grey and his beard was almost white. Apart from that and a few extra pounds in weight he had hardly changed since we met each other as teenagers. We had started our adventures together back in 1974 and the journey was still continuing. We filled our glasses and drank a toast to the bird.

A month after we moved in a card came under the door. It was from our neighbours across the road welcoming and inviting us to join them on Guy Fawkes night for their annual fireworks party. Jeremy was reluctant but I was keen to meet as many new people as I could so we went along and had a lovely evening. It was at this party that we were introduced to our neighbour Kate who lived further along the road on another smallholding. We stood chatting politely and then Jeremy asked, 'Do you have any livestock?'

'Of course. I keep a herd of pedigree Dexter cows and I have three Dales ponies.' Jeremy's antennae shot up.

'Do you have any spare manure that we could buy?'

'I've got tons of it and you can come and get whatever you want and we'll settle up later.' Kate had a smile on her face realising that she had found some willing customers to not only take away some of her muck mountain but were also willing to pay for it. We stood a while longer, drinking our beer and making the first steps in a getting to know you ritual with Kate which would continue over the next weeks and months. The following morning Jeremy walked down the road to make arrangements with Kate and later that day began the weekly chore of collecting cow and horse manure began in earnest. She was willing to let us come and fill our flimsy trailer as often as we wanted. However much we dug there was always plenty more to attack and Jeremy, as always, drove me on to take just another few spadesful. We put this black gold onto and into our soil and it enriched the ground and made it more productive than we could have imagined. In the course of all these visits down the road we became firm friends with Kate, although I am not at all sure what she made of these new townie neighbours nor, when I told her we were Jewish, our religious festivals and sabbaths, nor what she makes of us now!

We relocated to full time residence at The Gables in January 2014 and in the spring one morning Jeremy announced his new plan, 'Gill, we need some Dexters, like Kate.' As usual I was less enthusiastic than him but prepared to go along with his idea. Dexters are considerably smaller than Friesian dairy cows and are raised for their meat rather than as milkers. They are also beautiful cattle with good natures and the selling point for me was that we would have our own manure on site and the days of filling up the trailer would be over. Jeremy asked Kate to point us in the right direction, recommend some breeders and come with us to select two cows. By then we had paid a local contractor to fence all around the five acre field with post and rail fencing. The paddock, beside the house, had a thick, stock-proof hedge so there was no need to fence it. Kate, Jeremy and I set off one Sunday to visit the prize-winning herd belonging to Mr and Mrs Creasey which they kept just a few miles away. They had a selection of red and black Dexters and a number of young heifers – females who have not yet given birth to a calf. We had no idea which ones to choose. As we were casting our eyes over the herd and leaning on the gate Beatrix and Lucerne, one red calf and one black calf, sauntered over to speak to us. Into the field we went to take a closer look at the herd and make our choice but once again Beatrix and Lucerne pushed their way through and came to stand next to us. We didn't need a third sign. A price was negotiated and the owners said that they would deliver them in their trailer a few days later.

The day of delivery arrived and Kate joined us to watch the trailer being driven into the paddock and the heifers coming out into their new home. The grass was long and lush and the girls eagerly began munching. A few minutes later, as we sat in the dining room signing the paperwork, paying the bill and enjoying a cup of tea and a home-made biscuit our 'firework' neighbours across the road telephoned. 'Have you lost a black cow?' Paul asked, 'Because I have just seen one running down the road.' We all jumped up and ran out to the paddock and, to our dismay, only Lucerne was grazing on the grass and Beatrix was missing. Mrs Creasey who suffered from arthritis, remained with me in the dining room whilst Jeremy, Mr Creasey, Kate, Paul and Sharon and their children ran down the road after the cow. Our concern was not just for the cow but also for any unsuspecting drivers in their cars, lorries and tractors. As I sat with Mrs Creasey she shook her head and moaned, 'This has never happened in 30 years of selling cattle.' It wasn't funny but somehow her look, her voice and the vision of Beattie running away made me stifle a laugh and to this day the thought of that moment still makes me chuckle.

We were lucky. The cow was overtaken, turned around and directed back into the gate and the gap in the stock-proof hedge was located and temporarily fixed with a roll of wire that we had bought for a chicken run. Mr and Mrs Creasey were not sure about leaving their pedigree heifers with us, 'Are you sure you know how to look after cattle?' Mrs Creasey asked me. We persuaded them that we would really and truly take care of them and Mrs Creasey left, shaking her head and with grave misgivings.

We were now responsible for Beattie and Lucy and once you take on animals, even just two young cows, you might just as well take on some more and so we did.

When we lived in Devon back in the 70s I started listening to the Radio 4 daily soap opera drama, The Archers, 'an everyday story of country folk'. In those days, and from its early beginnings in January 1951, it addressed the lives and stories of a fictional village and managed to convey messages that would be of interest to farmers as well as the wider listening public. The story about Farmer Tony contracting lock jaw from a rusty nail made me go into Crediton town and get a tetanus jab. There was also a tale about Jacob sheep which were on the endangered species list.

Jacob sheep are mentioned in the Old Testament in the book of Genesis. The patriarch Jacob worked for seven years for his Uncle Laban in order to marry his younger daughter, Rachel. After a deception on the part of Laban, Jacob was married to the older daughter Leah following which he laboured as an unpaid shepherd for another seven years for his second bride, Rachel. His father-in-law asked what wages he wanted but Jacob said that he would be content to take as the brides' dowry all the striped and spotted sheep in the flock. Although Jacob sheep had not been present in Israel in modern times, tests have linked the breed to their Middle Eastern roots. In 2021 a Canadian farming couple moved to Israel taking with them 100 of their Jacob flock and reintroduced them to their ancient homeland.

Back in Devon we visited the weekly livestock market in Hatherleigh Market to see if we could find some of this biblical breed. We came back with two old ewes, Susie and Sybilla, who were missing several teeth, had four haphazard horns each but seemed content enough to live in our lower field. A few months later we added a ram, Uncle Laban, from the same market. We transported him home in the back seat of our car. He was a bad-tempered fellow who tried to butt me during the journey and later in the field. Laban was testosterone-fuelled and one morning, just as I was about to drive to work, our neighbour Farmer Isaacs called me and announced, 'Your ram has fair jumped over the hedge into our field, the bugger. Can you come and get him back.' I left our baby son strapped into his car seat while I hotfooted over to the field where the farmer, his two sons and I chased Laban out of their flock and back through the hedge to our land. I tied a log from a rope around the ram's neck which allowed him to walk and run but stopped him from jumping and escaping again. The following spring our neighbour's fluffy, white ewes gave birth to a number of black and white lambs. Luckily for us, Farmer Isaacs took it in good part, 'They all taste the same,' he said. Bless him.

Jacob wool was excellent for spinning and the skeins were unique in their colours and patterns. I spun on a New Zealand wheel and then hand-knitted jumpers for the three of us. Sadly, that spinning wheel was stolen from the garage of our London home several years before we moved to The Gables but I was keen to try my hand at the craft now that we were living in the countryside once again. We began our search for Jacob ewes.

Jeremy located a farm in Leicestershire that was advertising pedigree Jacobs for sale. The imposing house stood on a windy, but beautiful location near Naseby, the site of a famous English Civil War battle in 1645 when Oliver Cromwell's New Model Army defeated the Royalists. The farmer, selling the sheep, was actually a City accountant who, along with his wife, had bought and restored a derelict farm house and surrounding fields. He told us, 'I've a young fellow who works for me and he lives in a house on the farm with his wife and children.' It certainly was too big a place for just two people to manage.

To the side of the main house was an impeccable vegetable garden mostly set out in wooden raised beds. It was a perfect set up except for the chilling and constant wind, and I hoped that we were visiting on an unusually blustery day. The accountant invited us to climb into his blue Land Rover and off we roared to some fields a mile or so away where he kept his Jacob sheep. The vehicle raced over the uneven ground with me bouncing around in the back. It was fun and scary at the same time. We stood on the brow of the hill and admired the Jacobs grazing contentedly. Jeremy said to the owner, 'We'd like six of your sheep but we need you to deliver them as we haven't got a trailer.'

'That's fine but I'll have to charge you for the petrol and time.' That seemed reasonable to us. We had yet to own an animal trailer and many years on we still don't have one but instead make use of an ancient, ex-RAF Land Rover that saw service in Afghanistan.

Back at the estate the farmer took us to see some of his other rare breeds including a flock of Manx Loaghton sheep with their extraordinarily long horns and dark brown wool. The farmer told us that they, 'Taste delicious, lean and gamey. We always keep one or two in the freezer.' When we told him that we had been vegetarians for over fifty years he was not impressed. 'How on earth can you raise livestock and then not eat your animals?' It is a question we are often asked. We both feel comfortable with the way that we keep stock, giving them a good free-range life with an excellent diet, care and love. When the time comes to sell our animals we know that the males will usually go for meat and only some of the females will be kept for breeding but they won't be wasted, abused or neglected. We just don't want to eat them ourselves!

When we got back to The Gables Jeremy telephoned the farmer and asked him to add two more Jacobs to our order. In for a penny, in for a pound. We might as well have eight ewes and try to get the grass under control.

The sheep arrived the following week in a smart, silver trailer and the door opened and out jumped eight bouncy Jacobs. Six of them were from the hillside and the other two (who we named Pinky and Perky because Pinky had a pink tip to her nose) were, it seemed, from a different flock. The six sheep stayed together and the other two kept their own company. Once they were comfortable in their new surroundings and hadn't escaped from the recently refenced paddock, we let the sheep and the cows into the long grass in the big field. All the stock promptly disappeared from view as the neglected grass was as tall as trees. This was slightly disconcerting but we had faith that the wooden fencing would keep them on our premises and it did. I spent several hours with a bucket of sheep nuts, lying on the grass near the gate and holding out my hand towards the ewes calling, 'Come here girls. Come and get this lovely food.' No chance. They had just been moved and would take a few days to get used to their new home and to me.

So now we had two cows, eight sheep and wanted to bring in some chickens. The first task was to build a chicken run and a chicken house. A self-assembly kit was ordered and some stakes and chicken wire purchased. We had learnt the hard way that totally free-range hens made tasty snacks for canny foxes.

Back in the days when we lived in Devon we had a chicken shed and nesting boxes in our top field. The hens wandered around, free as birds, all day long until we fed them and shut them into the shed overnight.

One horrible afternoon I received a call at work from Jeremy who had arrived home early. 'Are you sitting down?' He asked me.

'No, of course not. Why?'

'I've got some bad news. I just went up to the field and found chicken carcasses everywhere. They're all dead!' By the time I got back from work we discovered that a few clever girls had hidden in the hedges of the house opposite and we and our neighbours managed to round them up and get them inside. That weekend we dug around the hen house to quite a depth, spread wire mesh on the ground which we re-covered with soil and built a chicken wire fence six feet high to keep chickens in and foxes out. We never lost another bird.

Although we were now living at The Gables, Jeremy was still working full time, driving to and from London several days a week. I had retired from running the office as one of us needed to be at home to keep an eye on the animals. It dawned on us that we needed some help around the place and we asked if anyone knew of an older person who might like some outdoor work for a couple of mornings a week. The young lad who had fenced the field told us that his mate's dad had recently retired and that he would mention the position to him. That very afternoon the wonderful Chris turned up, shook Jeremy's hand firmly and said, 'I'm your man.' Thus began a great working relationship and friendship that continues to this day. Chris had run his own smallholding for a few years when he was a young man. Hard as he worked it was almost impossible to make a living for a growing family on five acres and so he commuted to London for many years where he was a supervisor for road tarmac crews until he retired just as we were looking for a handyman. He has so many skills, woodworking and building and mending tools and machines. He liked the look of our second-hand, battered and bruised Kubota tractor that was sitting in the garage and he is a dab hand at changing the tiller to the cutter and back again and tilling the garden when we have pulled up last year's crops. When the little, Japanese machine threatened to give up the ghost a few years ago he even found a fellow in his village who was able to repair it and give it a second lease of life. Chris came into our lives and helped to build chicken runs and duck runs, fix gates and feed animals when we needed to spend a weekend in London.

Once I had stopped commuting I was ready to throw myself into local activities. I tried the tennis club in the nearby town of St Neots. The women were friendly and the coach gave me a refresher lesson and I passed muster. The problem was that I only wanted to play once a week and as soon as the members realised they had a possible new recruit for doubles they wanted me to play more often. I had work to do on the smallholding and in addition my left hip was becoming more and more painful and would eventually need to be replaced. I needed to look closer to home.

Although our village is small there were a number of regular activities taking place, amongst them a Saturday gardening club, a Friday evening History Society and a book club. One of the older and long-standing village residents paid us a visit soon after we moved into The Gables and, looking for new blood, invited me to come to the History Society the following Friday.

'I would love to come to the meetings,' I told her, 'But unfortunately I can't come on a Friday night as I'm Jewish and Friday night is the beginning of our Sabbath.'

'I quite understand. Actually, my husband is Jewish but he isn't religious at all.' Well, that was another surprise.

I might have liked the gardening club but because it got together on Saturdays I wouldn't be able to attend that either however the village magazine mentioned a walking group that met every Wednesday at the green triangle near St Denys Church. I decided to give it a try and, not knowing what to expect, I set off for the village and was greeted by a smiling woman in a large green raincoat who introduced herself as Heather. 'We walk for about an hour at a reasonable pace and we use the footpaths across the fields. We stay off the roads as much as possible,' Heather informed me. I was pleased that I had worn my welly boots rather than a pair of trainers. There were just two other walkers, both women of about my age and we strode off across the Country Park on my first foray. The Wednesday walk was to become a regular fixture in my week and the number of walkers ebbed and flowed although Heather was the mainstay and I was always pleased to see her and to play 'follow my leader'. Sometimes we were as many as eight and sometimes just two. Quite often there were as many dogs as walkers. The friendships that I made continued even when some of the regulars moved to other villages and then new walkers arrived to take their places and became friends.

Heather had been a primary school headmistress before she retired and her oversized mackintosh was her 'playground duty coat'. For over 30 years she had been walking the footpaths around and through the village and nagging and nudging the local council to mark the tracks with the distinctive green footpath signs. her view was, 'If we don't use the paths we will lose the footpaths.' We were happy to join her crusade.

The walking group was just what I needed to meet and make new friends and I was surprised at what a varied bunch we were. There was Carmen, a friendly, loud and opinionated Argentinian whose two daughters loved to visit the animals at The Gables. One of them went on to become a vet. Carmen could never control her mismatched dogs – a large Lurcher and tiny Jack Russell cross – and we walkers were forever getting tangled up in their leads as she fought to stop the Lurcher from chasing after rabbits and to coax the Jack Russell from digging his heels in and lying down. Elli, a proud Welsh woman, always arrived at the green with her white hair beautifully styled, wearing Hunter boots and fashionable clothes. She wouldn't have looked out of place in Country Life magazine. I enjoyed her tales of the expat life she had lived in Hong Kong and Venezuela several years before she settled in our village. She told me that Brits who have spent their working lives abroad often find it difficult to stay in one place once they retire and, sure enough, within a few years she and her husband were on the move again and have plans for a further relocation. Although they moved away from Colmworth we remain friends. I soon discovered that Heather was one of the linchpins of the village. She organized the monthly community lunches and coffee mornings at the church with her next door neighbour and good friend, Kate. She was a church warden and a member of the gardening club. At Christmas time she persuaded children to take part in a Nativity play and at Easter she set up a very popular chocolate egg hunt. 'If we don't get the children involved in the church then it really has no future at all,' she told me. There was no artifice with Heather. She spoke her mind but in the nicest possible way and if she asked for 'voluntary help' it was almost impossible to refuse. She and I became firm friends quite literally until her dying days.

Occasionally Pat, who lived in one of the upmarket barn conversions adjacent to the churchyard, walked with us but there was friction between him and some of the group and he decided to walk on his own every day eventually losing a lot of the excess weight that he was carrying. When he and his wife moved house there was a sigh of relief in some quarters but I never really understood or wanted to understand the cause of all the ferribles – minor arguments – that went on in the village and I was glad that our house sat outside the village boundary in its own, secluded plot of land where I could stay away from village politics. Other people joined the walking group to try it out. Some stayed, some moved away, one had a second baby and could no longer walk with us. The Wednesday walk was and remains an activity that I enjoy come rain or shine and through the walking I got to know the village, the footpaths, several of its residents, old and new, and quite a few of the local dogs.

Although I was nervous about revealing my identity I decided that this time right from the outset I would be out and open about my Jewishness. I didn't want to have to make up excuses about not joining in with events that took place on Friday nights or Saturday – the Jewish Sabbath.

Back in Devon, in the late 1970s, many local people led a very parochial life. Some hadn't even been to London, much less abroad. There was the fear that if we mentioned that we were Jews some of these people would even think we had horns! That may sound outrageous now in multicultural Britain where the internet and the television have opened our eyes to diversity but it really wasn't like that then. I remember one horrible incident when Daisy the cow was writhing in agony and unable to get up onto her feet. I called a vet and he arrived and announced that she had bloat, often a result of eating too much spring grass after a winter indoors. He rolled her over and released some of the gas and told me to put her in the stable and just let her out little by little until she got used to the fresh pasture. I was seven months pregnant, 23 years old and, that day, on my own at the Old Forge. The vet then proceeded to make a remark about not wanting black people to come and invade Devon like they had in London and then said something to the effect that all Jews were mean. To my shame, I was unable to confront this big, blustery fellow. I was intimidated by his age and authority but I am still angry with myself that I didn't have the guts to speak out.

Our Devon neighbour Mrs Isaacs the farmer's wife, had grown up in our house and her father had been the village blacksmith who shod all the local horses outside the annex to our cottage. We were always finding horseshoes as we dug in our vegetable garden and then hanging them on the wall, with the points of the shoe directed upwards for good luck. From time to time I would pop in with the baby to chat and have a cup of tea with Mrs Isaacs. I rarely understood much of what she said because of her thick Devon accent. I did my best. I was also wary of the two Jack Russell dogs that yapped and snapped at my ankles. Mrs Isaacs once confided to me that her two boys, both in their 30s and still living on the farm, 'Don't want to share a bed no more.' Jeremy, too, had experience of the old-fashioned practices of a few of his isolated country clients. One summer he was on a placement as a trainee social worker in rural North Devon. During some of the home visits he was shocked to find disabled and educationally challenged adults sitting all day long in the corners of rooms like guilty secrets. In the 1970s there was far less inclusion in schools and workplaces for the disabled than there should have been. Sadly, there are still too many physical barriers and prejudices placed in the way of the disabled and we have a long way to go before we can say that we live in a truly fair and equal society. In those days in Devon I worked as a physiotherapist in a school for children who were then called 'handicapped' and this was run by the Spastics Society. Today I shudder at the insensitivity of the name of what was, in the last century, a well-known and well- respected organisation and I am ashamed of the labels and limitations that this placed on the children. The Charity did not change its name to Scope until 1994. Society tolerated and even promoted prejudice against anyone who was different and many of us, Jews, Asians, Afro-Caribbeans, were all too aware of the overt racism and ignorance that existed all around the country. I wanted to keep my head down.

I soon realised that I couldn't hide from everyone when one Christmas Eve having drinks with all our neighbours across the road from The Old Forge in our tiny Devon hamlet one of them said to me, 'You're Jewish aren't you?' I don't know how he guessed but, of course, he was correct so there was no more pretending with my neighbours and that was a relief and neither John and Heather nor any of the others in the hamlet ever treated us differently once they knew that we were Jewish.

Being Jewish is an essential part of who I am and this time I had no intention of hiding my religion. I explained to my new friends in the village why I couldn't eat in their homes. Yes, I could have a cup of coffee, but no I couldn't eat their food as we kept kosher and in addition we were also committed vegetarians. All processed food has to be approved (or rejected) by a board of rabbis who send supervisors out to factories to check that the ingredients of the product are allowed by our religious law. If one knows where to look one can find the stamp from the religious authorities on some everyday items including plain Kettle crisps and Walkers shortbread biscuits and numerous factory-baked breads which states that the food is kosher. There are lists available online or in an annually updated booklet to let us know which processed foods we may or may not eat. My new friends were interested and a bit puzzled as to all the dietary regulations that we followed. This was hardly surprising as it is a very complicated subject even for those of us who adhere to its rules. They also revealed, much to our amazement, that there was another Jewish couple who had a weekend house in the village. They found it strange that this couple would break bread with them in their homes, whereas we would not. Like all religions there are different groups with stricter or more liberal views. In modern terminology we are all on a religious spectrum, from what one of my non-religious Jewish school friends calls a cultural Jew to those who try to keep every one of the 613 commandments laid down in the Old Testament. We frequently have ultra-orthodox Jewish visitors to The Gables from Stamford Hill and Golders Green and Gateshead who will not eat our food as they are not sure if they can trust our kosher credentials.

CHAPTER FIVE –
A FESTIVAL OF FREEDOM AND CONFINEMENT

Our lives, as observant Jews, are governed not only by the weekly Sabbath but also by the cycle of festivals in the yearly calendar.

Four weeks after the celebrations of Purim comes the festival of Passover when Jews mark their escape from slavery in 1300 BCE. It is an eight-day festival which involves a great deal of upheaval. When I explained what we do to Kate she said, 'That's mad. You do all of that for just one week of the year.' Several walkers, Elli and Heather, were similarly astonished as are many of my less religious Jewish friends and even my own brother. What is it that is so crazy?

Moses led the Children of Israel out of Egypt following the punishment of the ten plagues that persuaded Pharaoh to obey Moses's famous request, 'Let my people go.' The families fleeing Egypt were unable to wait for their bread to rise and they took flat, unleavened bread – called Matza – with them to eat on the journey. Because of this we don't eat any bread or flour or any risen products or those that contain leaven during the eight days of the festival. There is meticulous cleaning of our houses from top to bottom and foods forbidden for Passover are stored and locked away. I suppose this is similar to spring cleaning but the difference is that we have a time limit which ends the night before the festival begins. My kitchen cupboards never look as clean or tidy the rest of the year and it is a great opportunity to check expiry dates on tins and packets and to find things that were thought to be lost but were really lurking at the back of a drawer.

To ensure that we keep these rules we change every pot and pan, knife and fork, cup and saucer in our kitchens. Yes, we really have a completely different set of utensils and crockery for Passover and we get these out for just eight days a year. We are vegetarians and this means that we only have one set of dishes and pots and pans for everyday and Passover use. But…if we ate meat then we would need two sets of crockery and utensils for both daily and Passover use. How so? It says in the book of Exodus that 'you shall not seethe a kid in its mother's milk.' From this we derive the strict dietary laws that meat and milk products should neither be cooked together in the same pan nor eaten together at the same meal on the same plates. Ergo religious Jews need two sets of everything in their kitchens to keep meat and milk products separate. Two sets for daily use and two sets for Passover. At Purim time, four weeks earlier, I regularly receive a forwarded photograph on Whatsapp of a woman drinking an oversized glass of wine. The caption reads, 'Drink to forget that Passover is only four weeks away!' No wonder we drink at Purim when we think of the all the upheaval to come.

Observing Passover at The Gables was going to be difficult. The traditional Seder meal, which begins the festival, is a huge family affair and one of the events that even non-observant Jews generally make an effort to attend. Our annual plan was to stay in London and be with family for the Seder nights and invite guests to The Gables for the other days when families like to go on Matza picnics and outings. As the festival often coincides with Easter and school holidays it works well for parents and children and The Gables and its newborn lambs is a fun place to visit during Passover. This pattern was broken for us and everyone else in 2020 when the Covid pandemic forced huge changes to all our lives.

The day before lockdown our daughter Rosa, son-in-law, grandson and my niece threw all their most treasure possessions into two cars, emptied their fridges and food cupboards, grabbed their Sabbath candlesticks and phone and laptop chargers and arrived at The Gables for who knew how long. I said to Rosa, 'I think this could be the end of the world as we know it.'

'Mum, you're being a bit melodramatic. But if you're right then at least we're in the right place to sit it out. You and dad can teach us how to grow our own food.'

My niece Lucy was enthusiastic. 'I'll help you with the animals. I love animals. You and Uncle Jeremy can have a lie-in at the weekends and I'll let the chickens out and feed the goats.' That all sounded marvellous. In the following three months not one of our lodgers lifted a finger in the garden nor did anything with the animals other than stroke them! I had gone into complete survivalist mode which I had been prepared for since I lived in Devon all those years ago during the Cold War when Russia and America were sabre-rattling with nuclear weapons and I was an active member of the Campaign for Nuclear Disarmament. Now we were hiding from an invisible virus in The Gables bunker.

A year after we had moved to The Gables Jeremy was keen to restore the barn and stable block. He had to work hard to persuade me and I resisted the project for several months as I worried about the cost and the disruption. Once the building work started I was excited about the space it would offer for entertaining and the extra bedrooms for overnight guests. During lockdown we appreciated the barn conversion more than ever. When we designed the reconstruction of the courtyard we put in a second kitchen so that we could cater for our expected guests without walking to and from the house. We had four self-contained bedrooms opposite the barn and each of those was fitted with its own shower and toilet. The refugees had their space and we had ours and, given that there were some strong personalities and a great deal of uncertainty in the air, we avoided too many major clashes between us and them.

It was just a few weeks before Passover and this was going to be a Seder night with a difference. Most of the families that we knew in London and Manchester were having difficulty in buying eggs which are a traditional component of the meal. Here in the countryside, those of us with chickens had no shortage. Spring is when chickens come back into lay after a go-slow during the cold, dark winter months. We had enough eggs and then some. Fortunately we had put broadband into the barn soon after we completed the restoration and Rosa worked in there, whilst son-in-law sat in the house lounge sharing the internet with Jeremy who worked in his office next to the kitchen. Lucy sat at a desk in one of the annex bedrooms and our grandson took part in Zoom lessons and in between times his parents took it in turns to supervise his assignments and homework. The ten-year old did not see another child in person for 12 long weeks. When grandson got fed up he would call out, 'Who's taking me on my country walk today?' Then one of us, usually his mum or me, would put on our walking boots and take him for a good long stretch across the fields. Grandson learnt his way around the footpaths and became, at ten years old, a much faster walker than me and I regularly had to ask him to, 'Slow down, please.' It was a pleasure to have him with us although he missed his friends and we missed our two younger grandchildren who we Face-Timed but didn't see for nearly three months. Niece Lucy reorganised all the activities and programmes that had been planned for the youth organisation that she headed. Jeremy carried on advising divorcing couple without knowing when or where they would be able to attend court. My life remained much the same but without any help from the weekly gardener I was cutting the grass and hedges myself as well as tending the fruit and vegetable gardens. Our lovely Wednesday morning friend and cleaner, Dianne, wasn't allowed to work so there was additional housework as well as arranging Friday night dinners in the house. We discovered that eating together every evening didn't work for any of us as we all had different schedules. The refugees from London did their own thing and we did ours and we met up for Sabbath meals once a week. Perfect. Then there was Passover and we all pulled together. Son-in-law meticulously cleaned the barn kitchen and put away the utensils. I cleaned the house. All of us got out the boxes of Passover cutlery and crockery from the upstairs cupboard and we managed to buy matzas and other Passover foods online which were delivered through one of the coveted supermarket slots. It was a privilege to be with family to hold our Seder at The Gables when so many had to sit alone at their tables eating the symbolic foods from the Seder plate, the unleavened bread and drinking the four cups of wine. We will never forget those strange days, weeks and months.

CHAPTER SIX –
SHAVUOT AND SHEEP TAILS

Seven weeks on from Passover there is the harvest festival of Shavuot – Pentecost – and in June 2014, less than a year after we bought The Gables we attempted our first big gathering for friends and family.

This is a two-day festival which celebrates the giving of the ten commandments to Moses on Mount Sinai 49 days after the Exodus from Egypt. We typically eat cheese and cheesecakes at Shavuot possibly because, amongst many other suggested reasons, it is spring time when cows and goats are eating fresh pasture and producing an abundance of milk. It is traditional to stay awake all night at the beginning of the festival as if we, ourselves, were preparing for the Almighty to hand us the ten commandments just as he did to Moses on Mount Sinai. At The Gables we sat around the dining room table and several of the group delivered short lectures on subjects relating to the festival and other religious topics. In between talks I brought tea and refreshments to the participants which helped to keep everyone alert and happy.

We had planned for this first Shavuot festival since we arrived at The Gables. The triple garage had been converted into three bedrooms and bathrooms but the barns and stables were out of bounds and dangerous. We hired two cottages on the nearby golf course, about a 15 minute walk away, and one family of six pitched a tent on the front lawn. Somehow or another we accommodated 25 adults and 12 children, including my mother-in-law in her wheelchair with her two kind and efficient Filipino carers. For the two weeks leading up to Shavuot I had asked the builder, 'Will the rooms be ready in time?'

Every day he assured me, 'Don't worry it will be fine.' A week before the festival the builder brought in his 15 year old son and they worked all night, plastering and then painting the walls. My nerves were shredded. Then there were the frantic calls to the chief executive of UK Power Network to get the electricity to the annex connected and switched on. I begged, I pleaded and played the disabled mother-in-law card and we made it. The power to the rooms went live. Then we realised, at the 11ᵗʰ hour, that one fridge would not be big enough for all the food and a second upright was ordered and delivered and plonked into the kitchen just in time for the festivities. As people arrived and the dishes of food piled up alongside crisps and dips, cheese cakes and fruit, I quite literally threw up my hands shouting out, 'I can't cope!'

Son-in-law, a seasoned organiser, cook and one time youth leader turned to me and said, 'Gill, just make yourself a cup of coffee and then get out of the kitchen and let me sort it.' Within half an hour he had found a place for all the food. We used the lounge for the synagogue services and then, with a quick turnaround, put up extra trestle tables along the length of the room so that 37 of us could sit down for the meals. I am still amazed that with so many adults and little children not one bowl of soup was spilt on the carpet nor any dishes broken. It was a great success and, as I wrote on my blog on June 6, 2014, *'Two wonderful days. 25 adults, 12 children, enough food to feed a small army and…we did it. A group effort with everyone serving food, looking after each other's children, clearing the kitchen and washing up, feeding the cows and sheep more times than they should be fed, watching the barn owl circle the field in the evening sunshine, walking in the rain, playing on the climbing frame, cuddling crying children and making them smile again, watching the baby charm everyone especially her 87 year old great grandmother and 93 year old great grandfather.'*

Two years later, at another gathering at The Gables to celebrate Shavuot, we were able to accommodate all our friends and family on our own premises. By then we had restored the wooden beamed barn and converted the stables around the courtyard into four more bedrooms. Most of us had stayed up all night, learning and studying, eating and drinking and then recited the morning prayers as the day broke. After a few hours' sleep we reconvened in the barn to drink wine and whisky, partake of crisps and crackers and savoury dips before a country walk and a festive lunch. Whilst our guests chatted Jeremy and I made our usual round of the animals, checking their hay and water. We noticed that several of the sheep were jumping around and twitching and trying to scratch their behinds on the fences and gates. Taking a closer look we saw, to our horror, that two of the sheep had maggots crawling around in their flesh. As it was a Holy Day I couldn't use the telephone to call the vet nor could I switch on my computer and consult Dr Google.

'I'm going over to Kate's,' I said to Jeremy, 'You look after the guests. She might know what to do.'

I ran down the road and when I found Kate she didn't like the sound of the sheeps' condition. Knowing that I couldn't use the telephone, she decided to call Farmer Rob who had a great deal of experience with sheep. He told Kate that he would be with us as soon as he could. This was to be the first of our many meetings and dealings with Rob, who has helped us now for many years. I'm sure that Rob must have been surprised to find a group of 30 people standing around drinking whisky and wine and snacking at 11 o'clock on a midweek morning but he hid his reaction well. Jeremy and I had donned our work coats and wellingtons whilst our guests were all in their festival finery and we left them in the barn as we took Rob to the sheep shed where he expertly examined the girls.

'These two,' he said 'Have a serious case of blow fly.'

'What's that?' I hadn't heard of it before nor seen it on any of our livestock when we lived in Devon

'The flies are attracted to the dung that accumulates around the back end of the sheep, especially ones like yours whose tails haven't been docked. They lay their eggs in the wool which hatch into maggots. The maggots burrow into the flesh to feed and can quite quickly kill the sheep.'

'Can you save them?' I was practically in tears.

'I'll certainly try. I've brought my clippers and I'm going to shave all around the infected areas and then spray them. That should kill off the maggots. I'll come back in a couple of days and spray all the sheep with another chemical which prevents any more flies from hatching.'

Rob worked deftly and skilfully and within a short space of time he had removed the parasites and treated the animals and we took him over to the barn where he washed his hands and then joined us for a tot of whisky. I wondered, as I so often have, at the strange events that take place at The Gables even as we manage to celebrate the Sabbaths and festivals surrounded by nature and all that can and does occur in a rural setting. Jewish law insists that we feed and care for our animals before we look after ourselves. In the seminal daily prayer, the Shema, animal welfare features in the second of the prayer's three paragraphs. Farming and religion can definitely live side by side and that is what we hoped to achieve at The Gables.

40 years earlier when we lived in Devon in the late 1970s, sheep farmers were legally obliged to dip their sheep annually in organophosphate pesticides which killed off bugs and pests and so prevented blow fly strikes. Jeremy used to help Farmer Isaacs and his sons to dip their sheep in the toxic bath of chemicals in return for allowing us to put our Jacobs in with their flock. These organophosphates not only killed parasites but also poisoned hundreds if not thousands of farmers and were finally banned from general sale in 2002 and from manufactured products in 2007 in the UK and in 2012 across the EU. This was too late for the many who quietly suffered and still suffer the effects of these chemicals to this day.

We had shared the cost and care of three Jersey calves, Daisy, Bluebell and Clover which we bought from an organic farmer, Mark Purdey, who lived on a piece of land not far from our Devon home. Mark was a gentle and thoughtful giant of a man. As his obituary in the Daily Telegraph wrote in 2006, he was '*born in Much Hadham, Hertfordshire to a long line of gifted eccentrics. An ancestor of his ...walked from Inverness to London to set up Purdey's gunsmiths.*' The Guardian wrote of Mark, '*He was educated at Haileybury College before turning down a place at Exeter University initially embarking on a kind of post hippie bucolic existence...and ran a dairy farm in Devon.*'

Mark was also a saxophone player and he persuaded me to join him and other lay musicians to play jazz at the home of a friend in the nearby village of West Sandford. My violin playing was definitely not up to their standard but I enjoyed hearing and watching them jam and I later learnt that Mark would play his saxophone on his farm to calm his cows. When we knew this lovely man he was in between wives and teetering on penury. He would arrive at our house driving his tractor (he couldn't afford a car) which he parked in our yard and then would dine with us around our wooden kitchen table. Sometimes he was so tired that after

JEWS MILK GOATS

a meal and a couple of glasses of scrumpy he would bed down in our lounge for a few hours of sleep before returning home to care for his beloved herd.

In 1982 when all farmers in England and Wales were compelled to used Phosmet – an organophosphate compound – to prevent the spread of an outbreak of warble fly amongst cattle, Mark went to court to oppose the order. He believed that these chemicals, which had been created before World War II as a nerve gas, would compromise his highly prized organic Jersey milk. By the time the case came to the High Court for judicial review Jeremy and I and our two young children were back living in North London. Mark and his Devon solicitor, a mutual friend named Pete Ward slept on the floor of our small house in East Finchley the night before the court case. Jeremy, a newly qualified solicitor, was Mark's London agent. On the day of the case Jeremy described how a campaign group supporting Mark walked up and down Fleet Street dressed as pantomime cows. The case was settled on the steps of the High Court and Mark did not have to spray his cows with the chemicals. Instead he was allowed to use a less toxic compound which had the same anti warble fly effect. In later years Mark became a self-taught expert on organophosphates and their possible implication in the spread of BSE, Bovine Spongiform Encephalopathy colloquially known as mad cow disease. He wrote learned papers on the subject and lectured widely. The then Prince of Wales, now our King Charles, took a great interest in this work as did Lord King, the former defence minister. Ted Hughes the poet laureate at the time was a long-term friend and supporter. Tragically Mark died from a brain tumour at the age of 52 but his ground-breaking work changed farming practices here in the UK and around the world.

The spray that Farmer Rob used to kill the flies on our sheep definitely did not contain the toxic organophosphates that were banned thanks to the work of the late Mark Purdey, who I am proud to have known. I am pleased to say that we have avoided any further fly strikes in subsequent years.

58

CHAPTER SEVEN –
CELEBRATIONS AND CONDOLENCES

Two days after our first big gathering for Shavuot 2014, on a bright June Sunday, we opened The Gables once again for the very special occasion of my parents' 65th Wedding Anniversary. Tables and chairs were set up outside in the glorious sunshine and as the guests arrived, we greeted Mum and Dad's friends who had driven up from London to celebrate with our family. There was an abundance of food laid out on the dining room tables including platters of bridge rolls and bagels filled with cream cheese, smoked salmon and egg. The fish, although not vegetarian fare, was a concession to my parents and they appreciated the gesture. There were plates of Danish pastries and cream-filled patisserie, dishes of exotic fruits and two anniversary cakes. It was a unique setting for a party and when Dad stood up and declared, in front of all their friends and family, 'How much I love you, Sybil,' the Dexter cows and Jacob sheep wandered past in the background as if on cue. Champagne was popped and everyone wished mum and dad and each other, 'Mazel Tov!' – congratulations. It was a beautiful and memorable day for an exceptional couple.

Three weeks after their anniversary, during a world cup football match on the television, Dad felt tired and told Mum that he was going to bed early. Forty-five minutes later Mum went into the bedroom to find Dad on the bed still fully dressed. He had collapsed and passed away completely painlessly and peacefully in his own home with his beloved wife. We were grateful that we had managed to celebrate 65 years in such fine style and that dad had exited this world so gracefully without becoming an invalid. There were no regrets just a lifetime of wonderful memories, fantastic experiences and albums of photographs.

Jews bury their dead very quickly, usually within a day or two. This is followed by a week of mourning, called the Shiva – the Hebrew word for seven – for the immediate family. My non-Jewish friends had always been amazed at the way that Jewish people managed to gather together for a funeral often with less than a day's notice. In one of the paragraphs at the beginning of our daily prayer book it states, *'These are the things whose fruits we eat in this world but whose full reward awaits us in the World to Come: honouring parents, acts of kindness, arriving early at the house of study morning and evening, hospitality to strangers, visiting the sick, helping the needy bride, attending to the dead, devotion in prayer and bringing peace between people…'* These commands are taken seriously from generation to generation.

Dad's sudden passing was not without its humorous moments. My mother, who always got Dad to drive her to her weekly hairdressing appointment, had been persuaded by a friend to book a hairdresser to come to her flat the week that Dad died and the hairdresser was due the following morning. Dad was lying in their bedroom overnight from where the bearers from the Jewish Burial Society were going to arrive to collect his body and take it to the cemetery until the funeral. As Mum and I sat in her lounge on the night of Dad's passing trying to sleep, Mum suddenly remembered the home appointment. 'Oh my goodness,' Mum said putting her hand over her mouth and stifling a laugh, 'This is like some sort of black comedy. I can't let the hairdresser come here tomorrow. We must phone and cancel her. She's due to be here in the morning.'

'Don't cancel her Mum, you'll want your hair to look nice for the levoye.'

'You're right. I'll leave it as it is.'

As we finished our breakfast mugs of coffee the doorbell rang. I opened it and said, 'Hello, you must be Michelle. I'm Sybil's daughter. Mums in the lounge because Dad passed away last night and dads in the bedroom.'

The poor woman's face fell and she looked startled.

'I'm so sorry. I'll leave you and come another time.'

'Oh no, please don't go. Mum needs to have her hair looking nice for the funeral.'

To her credit Michelle walked into the flat and I ushered her into the second bedroom at the end of the corridor closing the door to mum and Dad's bedroom so that she didn't catch sight of Dad's covered body.

Whilst the hairdresser got to work on Mum's hair the doorbell rang for a second time. This time it was the bearers arriving to take dad's body to the cemetery. I opened the front door, asking them to, 'Please wait a second,' whilst I ran to close the door to the temporary hairdressing parlour. It didn't seem respectful to let them see Mum having her hair done just a few hours after Dad had passed away. The bearers picked Dad up gently and carried him out on a stretcher to their ambulance. I breathed a sigh of relief, opened all the doors and offered Michelle and Mum a cup of tea.

Later that day, after the funeral service, I returned to Mum's flat where Mum, my brother and I sat on low chairs passing the time with visitors who came to give us comfort, chat about Dad, talk about the old days and joined us in the evening as we recited memorial prayers. In the week of mourning the immediate mourners are not expected to cook or work and people bring food to the Shiva house. The seven days is a transition time for the family of the deceased before they have to return to daily life. I stayed in London for the week whilst Jeremy drove up and down the road each morning and afternoon, looking after the livestock and then joined us for the evening prayers at Mum's flat.

I didn't have time to explain to my new Colmworth friends about a Shiva and I wouldn't have expected them to come and visit me in London, but eight years after that when Mum died, it was a different situation.

Dad was 86 when he died. Mum, also 86, continued to live independently and enjoyed her afternoon games of bridge playing with other widows. Four years later she said to me, 'Whoever thought that I would live so long? Now that I'm 90 I know I'm losing the plot. I'm going to stop playing bridge before I embarrass myself and my friends at the card table and I think I'll need some help at home.'

We were blessed to find a carer, the lovely Olga, who spent five mornings a week with Mum, but then the nights became difficult and Mum often had to activate the emergency button she wore around her neck. My brother would drive to her flat, often in the early hours of the morning, and help Mum get up from the floor and back into bed. We invited Mum to live with us at The Gables. She declined saying, 'It's too far from my friends and the grandchildren. I'd be bored. Let's go and visit some care homes where I'd have some company.'

We saw two unsuitable places but the third home was run by the charity Jewish Care and it was a beautiful, new building set on a 15 acre site on the edge of North London. She and I both knew that this was the place for her and when the interview with the facilities manager ended mum put her hands together and said out loud, 'I just pray that I can get a place here.' Within a week a room became available and Mum accepted it without hesitation and moved to Anita Dorfman House in November 2019.

Jewish Care is a charity that runs over 70 centres and services which includes care homes for the elderly. The organisation has evolved from the Jewish Board of Guardians which was founded in London in 1859 to care for poor and infirm Jewish immigrants arriving in England from Russia in the 19th century. Later in the 20th century it became known as the Jewish Welfare Board. In 1990 the Jewish Blind Society merged with the Jewish Welfare Board and was renamed Jewish Care which is one of the 100 largest UK charitable organisations ranked by annual expenditure. As former Chancellor Sajid Javid said about the charity, 'One thing that distinguishes the Jewish community is the way you look after each other in so many ways.' It may be that we Jews, as outsiders, have always needed to help ourselves. The Old Testament commands us to look after widows and orphans, the sick and the poor and to give tzedakah – charity. Even if we don't have much to give, we have an obligation to help those less fortunate than ourselves.

All Jewish Care facilities provide kosher food and there are Sabbath and Festival services in all the residential homes which means that there is a heimishe – homely – environment for their residents and that certainly helped Mum to feel comfortable as she settled in.

For the first six months Mum was happy and content in her room with its ensuite bathroom and front facing window. She sat at a table of four in the dining room, enjoyed the food and made many new friends. I visited her every week as did my brother and many of her old friends. Then in March 2020 life for all of us, but especially for the elderly in care homes, was tragically and brutally shut down. The care staff were obliged to wear masks and gloves and suddenly we were not allowed into the home anymore. Our visits became window stops with us standing on one side of the glass speaking to Mum on the phone as she peered out and waved at us and at her great grandchildren. It was a terrible sadness for everyone and we watched mum try to put on a brave face although she couldn't always contain her distress. As national restrictions eased the family took regular Covid tests and were allowed inside under strict controls. I would go into Mum's room, sneakily close the door and slip off my mask and Mum and I would find a way to make each other laugh but each time my brother and I saw her our hearts would break. Mum's beloved great grandchildren had to remain on the far side of the window until one very special day we were allowed to bundle Mum up in her winter coat and take her outside in a wheelchair. Then the two youngest great grandchildren held her hand and kissed her and mum smiled her wonderful smile and was finally happy again.

In February 2022 Mum had become a frail 94-year-old woman. As she would have said she was just skin and bone. She didn't want to eat and she no longer wanted to stay in this world. The exceptionally kind and truly caring staff allowed us all to visit and be with her day and night until the end and finally she was at peace. Covid was a cruel disease whose restrictions and repercussions were felt and are still felt by so many families.

Mum was buried within 48 hours in the outer London Bushey cemetery in the plot reserved for her next to Dad. I sat in mourning with my brother for one day in London and the rest of the week I sat Shiva at The Gables. I sent out an email to my local friends explaining the mourning rituals and let them know that they would be welcome to come in to see me and not to be nervous! It was touching that so many of these friends came to pass the time with me as I sat on a low chair in the lounge. Several of them brought flowers, which is not traditional in a Jewish house of mourning. The previous day Dianne had helped me cover all the mirrors throughout the house and that was the first strange thing that non-Jewish friends would notice. I explained to them, as I had to Dianne, 'When we're mourning we're not supposed to be concerned with our physical appearance. We wear slippers because in the olden days, leather shoes were more comfortable than other footwear. I also have to wear the same clothes during the week that I wore at Mum's funeral.' I showed my friends Annmarie and Judy the customary cut that had been made in my jumper and dress on the day of the funeral. 'It symbolises the rending of garments that grief-torn people would have carried out in days gone by. When a parent dies one of the funeral bearers cuts our outer garments towards the heart because the loss of a parent is so deep and heartbreaking.' Annmarie was nodding and so was Judy who was sitting next to her listening quite intently to my explanations. 'We're allowed to get up and bathe on Friday afternoon and change into our best clothes to honour the Sabbath.'

'Thank goodness for that,' said Judy, 'I should think you would really want a bath and a change after sitting in those clothes all week.'

'There's more too but I'll tell you about it another time'.

'I know some of it,' said Judy, 'Because I had a Jewish colleague when I worked in London and he didn't listen to music or go to parties for the year after his dad died.'

'That's true and we're not supposed to buy new clothes for a year after a parent dies. The mourning rules are stricter for a mother or father than for the loss of a spouse or sibling or even a child. But remember it all depends how observant someone is whether or not they keep all the rules and lots of Jewish people just keep some of the rules or maybe none of them.'

I introduced my Colmworth pals to those who had made the more than 50 mile journey from London to make condolence visits and I was really happy to see the two groups get to know each other in our living room at The Gables. My nephew had driven all the way from Brighton just to spend two hours with me and that was truly appreciated. A cousin of Jeremy's was struggling to walk but his wife and he drove here just to see me and reminisce. It was a great comfort and also, as Mum would have agreed, a sociable occasion, one to which I didn't have the invitation list so I didn't know who would turn up.

The locals found the Jewish way of death and mourning new and interesting. Annmarie asked, 'What about the actual funeral? How do you decide what prayers or hymns you want when you bury so quickly. There's no time really to work it out, is there?'

"That side of it is easy because the funeral service is the same for everyone. I've always liked the way that there's no difference between a millionaire or a pauper. We all get buried in simple white shrouds and in a plain, wooden coffin and the prayers are the same for everyone. Death truly is the great leveller. The only difference on the day is the eulogy.'

'The whole funeral business seems much easier when there's no arguments over the service or the casket,' Annmarie reflected afterwards.

As my Jewish visitors began to leave they stood in front of me and recited the customary words, 'I wish you long life.'

This was also strange to my non-Jewish friends. 'It's what we say to anyone who is bereaved and also on the anniversary of the death of a close relative. It's a bit like with the funeral service. We don't have to think about what to do, we just have a set formula which makes it easy.'

'Yes,' agreed Judy, 'We struggle to know how to greet someone if we see them in the street before or after our funerals. And we often wait several weeks before the funeral or cremation. Everyone is in a state of limbo.'

It was certainly an unusual house of mourning and may have been the only Shiva in England where people were able to go outside and cuddle newborn lambs and photograph each other doing so. I have several memorable pictures from those days of Shiva. There were more smiles than tears which is just what Mum would have wanted.

Mum passed away three days before the conflict in Ukraine began on February 24th 2022. For several weeks I had been driving up and down the A1 to visit Mum as she lay, bedbound and hardly able to talk. The radio in the car and my iphone alerts kept me abreast of the build-up of Russian tanks on the Ukrainian border and at times I felt torn between sitting quietly with mum, stroking her hand and arm when she became agitated and then trying to contact our friends in Ukraine. Like so many others here and around the world our family was in a state of turmoil over the start of the invasion. Jeremy and I had such close and strong connections with the Jewish community in Lviv and it is no exaggeration to say that I was heartbroken at both the loss of my mother and the conflict in Eastern Europe. As I sat in mourning I was also trying to stay in contact with Sara, the Rabbi's wife with whom I had been close friends for over 20 years. She and her husband and children were providing food and refuge in the synagogue for hundreds of people trying to escape to the nearby border with Poland. We were terrified for them, for the beautiful city of Lviv and for all the people of Ukraine.

CHAPTER EIGHT –
FELINE FRIENDS

Both Jeremy and I grew up in flats in central London. Although Jeremy's family owned a series of dogs the only pet my brother and I ever had was a goldfish that our dad won at the Hampstead Heath fair one bank holiday Monday. The fish took sick after three days of swimming in a glass bowl in the kitchen and Dad flushed it down the toilet and told us that it had gone to join the other fish out at sea!

My first proper pet was a cat we took into our home soon after we married. My relationship with Kitty was the start of my love affair with felines. In Devon our second cat, Muffin, had a great time chasing and killing mice and rats that she found in the animal feed barn. One warm, summer night as we were just falling off to sleep we heard a scuffling and excited mewing outside. It was Muffin on a night time kill and, looking for praise, she jumped onto the ledge above the front door and flung a half dead mouse in through our bedroom window. I screamed, 'Jeremy, get that out of here.' I kept on shouting as I stood on the bed and Jeremy chased the bloodied little creature around the floor until he managed to catch it, take it outside and put it out of its misery. We never slept with the window open again.

Later, when we returned to live in London our dog, Peggy, ruled our lives. She was a collie spaniel cross and she had the good nature of both breeds. The children's friends loved her and she charmed our neighbours and often took herself on unsanctioned walks to their houses for treats. We got used to her going missing and knew exactly where to find her. Sadly, as she aged, dementia set in and one day she disappeared and did not return. She had managed to creep out of the front door when we opened it earlier that evening and none of the neighbours had seen her. We called the nearest police station some five miles away. They had a dog that fitted Peggy's description. She had walked down to the busy main road near our house and crossed four lanes of traffic without getting run over. A kind gentleman had stopped his car and bundled the dog inside before she caused an accident. He took her to the police station where they logged her details and put her in a cage. Jeremy collected her that night, paid the fine and brought her home where we covered her with cuddles and kisses. The end was in sight. At the age of 16, she stopped eating, had to be carried up and down the stairs and one Thursday afternoon I drove her to the veterinary surgery. She lay cradled in my arms as the vet administered the injection that sent Peggy to her final resting place. Our house felt empty without her. Peggy's passing reminded me of an old Jewish joke. A priest, a vicar and a rabbi were debating the question, 'When does life begin?' The priest said, 'At the moment of conception.' The vicar said, 'When the foetus is viable.' The rabbi said, 'When the children leave home and the dog dies!' I began to understand that there were benefits to living without a pet. I wasn't tied to walking times and I didn't have to rush home to feed the dog. I felt liberated as well as sad when Peggy had gone.

Now, on our Bedfordshire smallholding, we had willingly taken on the responsibility for cows, sheep, a variety of chickens, four large Embden geese and two chatty call ducks.

The numerous birds were fed with a diet of corn and layers mash. The pellets scattered around the chicken runs were attracting mice and rats a-plenty. We seriously needed a pair of cats to control the rodents before the problem got out of hand.

We approached Cats Protection, a UK charity dedicated to rescuing and rehoming stray, unwanted or homeless cats. The organisation was founded in 1927 with the longer name of The Cats Protection League and over the years it has attracted an enormous income from donors and more recently through a chain of shops that are largely run and staffed by unpaid volunteers. In 2022 Cats Protection overtook the Dogs Trust charity in the amount of money they were gifted in legacies. The charity received £55 million from donations and legacies and £25 million from fundraising and another £1 million from the charity's investments. Britain truly is a nation of animal lovers.

We assumed that the local branch of the charity would be delighted with our offer of a place for their unwanted cats. Not so. We needed to be vetted, to have a home visit and then to wait anxiously, hoping for a positive report. Luckily, after the inspection and form filling, we were deemed to have suitable premises and the right attitude to cats. A few weeks later two fierce looking cat women, clad in combat trousers and black Doc Marten boots arrived, with a large cage, three feeding bowls and a comfort blanket for the occupants – a fluffy black male and a sleek haired, smaller female. The felines came with the names Mack and Mabel and we were ordered to keep them in the cage for at least a week until they had adjusted to their new surroundings. I am a great believer in the butter on the paws method of getting cats to adapt to their new home but the cat ladies disapproved of my plan. 'That's not the way we do it,' they told me sternly. 'And if you are thinking of doing that we will take the cats back right away.' The cat women were not for crossing! The butter theory is that by the time the cat has cleaned its paws sufficiently it will have worked out where it is and won't get lost.

We had used this method when we left London the first time and taken our marvellous tabby cat, Muffin, to our thatched cottage in Devon. My friend Eve and I had driven Jeremy's old Saab estate to our new home in the West Country. The back of the car was filled with pot plants and cleaning implements and a cat roaming free. She should have been in a cat carrier, but we didn't possess one. Every time we stopped for a coffee or a comfort break on the motorway I turned to Eve and called out in a panic, 'Hold onto the cat,' before I opened the driver's door. Only one of us at a time could leave the car while the other remained in the vehicle with Muffin. It was a hot, summer day and throughout the long drive we had to keep the windows tightly shut at all times. We arrived sweating and flustered at our new home, The Old Forge. Whilst Eve kept hold of Muffin I jumped out and made sure that all the house windows and doors were securely closed before my friend carried the tabby into the living room and shut the door behind her. Then we set to work unpacking the plants and cleaning gear, washing sinks, the bath and toilet and sweeping the floors. It was thirsty, dusty work and we decided to stop for a cuppa and put our feet up in the living room. We opened the door. The cat was nowhere to be seen. 'This is ridiculous.' I was running my hands through my hair and Eve could see that I was close to tears. 'She's got to be here. After that journey we just can't lose her now. I simply can't bear it.' I was becoming hysterical.

'Sit down, Gill. We're not going to get anywhere if you get yourself into a state. I'm sure she'll turn up and when the boys arrive we'll find her.' She was right. There was nothing more to be done and we finished our tea, carried on cleaning and when the boys eventually parked the removal van we resumed our fruitless search for Muffin. We were all exhausted and hungry. I would have to accept that Muffin had gone.

In the morning I went into the living room. As I opened the door a long, fluffy tail disappeared up into the chimney of the inglenook fireplace. The cat, feeling nervous and unsettled, had hidden there amidst the chaos of the move. Jeremy tempted her down with some food, put a good amount of butter on her paws and let her go out into the garden. By the time the butter had been licked away Muffin was relaxed and calm and she never disappeared again.

That cat was a wonderful companion who used to sit on Jeremy's shoulder like a parrot, catch mice and rats by the basket load and accompanied us on walks for a mile or two until she got bored. Sadly, just before we returned to London, she was run over on a sharp bend at the bottom of Stoneshill. She had negotiated the quiet roads for over four years and her lack of concentration was completely out of character. I always believed that she hadn't wanted to return to city life and had decided to make a grand exit before we moved.

Forty years later at The Gables our two black cats, Mack and Mabel, were soon out of their confinement and began hunting in earnest. Shrews, mice and moles and the occasional young rat were all fair game. The rabbits, that had plagued the vegetable patch and eaten celery and brassica seedlings, disappeared from the garden once they realised that Mabel could outrun them. Several times she turned up at the back door with a bunny hanging from her jaws and once I watched her race across the garden and catch a rabbit running, unsuccessfully, for its life. We weren't sorry to see the back of the rabbits and the garden thrived. Pigeons learnt to keep their distance or end up as teatime treats for Mack and Mabel. The cats were allowed some time in the house but they always slept outdoors at night in the Cat Barn bedding down in cardboard boxes lined with blankets, newspapers and an old sheepskin.

One day a tabby cat appeared at the back of the barn. It was scrawny and crying. I took it into the wooden shelter and gave him some food. He ate it ravenously. Then I told him, 'Off you go Mister, away home with you.' He wouldn't leave. A few days later I made an appointment to take Jose (named for Jose Mourinho the Manchester United football coach at the time) to the vet to see if he had a microchip and if we could find his owners. The vet confirmed that there was no microchip and not much hope of finding the owner. 'The cat seems to be very young. It was probably abandoned at the side of the road. People do that you know. If they don't want to keep kittens they often just throw them out of a car and let them take their chances. By the way your cat isn't a boy he's a girl.'

'Oh dear. I better change her name to Josie then and please can I book her in to be neutered as soon as possible?'

An appointment was made for the operation and Josie and I returned to the surgery the following Thursday. Later that day, the vet called to tell me that Josie was pregnant and asked what I wanted him to do. We agreed on a termination. By now the bills were mounting for this little cat but I was also falling in love with her.

One summer afternoon Mum, Jeremy and I were sitting out in the garden. There was a screech of brakes and Jeremy ran to the back gate to see what had happened. A shocked driver had pulled his car to the side of the road and lying there on the tarmac was Mack. 'I'm so sorry,' said the stricken motorist, 'He just ran straight out in front of me and there was nothing I could do.'

'It's not your fault. Our cats are always running across the road. It was bound to happen sooner or later.'

Cats and traffic are never good companions. We carried Mack into the garden on a makeshift stretcher of wood and Josie and Mabel licked him and sat with him as he moaned in agony. It was pitiful to watch him in pain but comforting to see the way that Mabel and Josie stayed by his side. After a phone call to the emergency vet, an animal ambulance arrived to collect Mack and take him in for appraisal and treatment. The kind driver and his wife took Mack into the ambulance and made him as comfortable as possible. All we could do was wait.

Two hours later I took a call from the vet. 'Mrs Freedman I'm sorry to say that Mack is badly injured. We've sedated him so he's not in pain but his back is broken. I could try to operate on him but I am not sure if he will ever be able to walk again. What would you like me to do?'

'I don't think that I want Mack to go through surgery if he won't be able to walk again. What do you think?'

'I agree Mrs Freedman, the best plan would be to put him to sleep without any further interference. Will you be wanting his ashes?'

'No that won't be necessary. Thank you for being honest with me and thank you for looking after him.'

I couldn't imagine Mack with a broken back being wheeled around on some sort of trolley contraption if such a device even existed. As much as I loved him I was not prepared to be a nursemaid to a cat. I focused on the happy times with Mack and tried to forget the last sad hours of his life.

Although Mack was no longer with us we still had the two cats, Mabel and Josie. Then one day, as suddenly as she had arrived, Josie disappeared. We hunted everywhere, asked the neighbours across the road to check their sheds and sent messages to friends in the village. No one had seen her. I put notices on lamp posts and on social media and went to see a cat matching her description in a neighbouring village. It wasn't Josie and I returned home disappointed. I continue to hope that she has found a better home and is living a life of luxury. There was now just one precious cat.

Heather called me a couple of weeks after Josie disappeared. 'Gill, have you got any spare cat food? A little, black cat has turned up in our yard. He doesn't want to leave. We think he might have come in the back of van when Brian had some ride-on mowers delivered to the workshop, but we just don't know. He's crying and hungry and I haven't got anything to feed him.' Even before I had time to leave the house Heather changed her mind and decided to take the cat to the vet to see if he was microchipped and whether they could find his owner. The cat didn't have a chip and the vet took him into the surgery cages for a week and advertised his whereabouts on social media to see if anyone would claim him. The veterinary nurses took a shine to their newest waif and christened him Nigel (could it been after Nigel Farrage? We never asked). At the end of the week, unclaimed, we were allowed to adopt Nigel. I was so scared that Nigel would disappear that I bought him a little cat harness and lead, which looked ridiculous, and walked him around the garden for several days before I allowed him to run free, with butter on his paws of course. The vet had told us that Nigel was a small cat. No, Nigel was a hungry cat and he ate and grew and ate and grew until he was a huge, sleek boy twice the size of Mabel. His purr was the sound of our tractor engine and he loved being stroked and petted. He was also a brilliant hunter and a skilled tree climber, often shinning up the ash tree in the front garden to stalk pigeons. Nigel became, and still is, a much loved, often naughty and always hungry character at The Gables. He is quite often the subject and star of the Gables blog that I write and he has a small fan club who comment on his antics. All food must be hidden away when Nigel is about. Recently he learnt how to open the butter dish and even the oven. Nothing is safe. He eats potato peel and cucumber and really just about everything that a discerning feline would ignore. The two cats rub along quite well together although Mabel often finds Nigel's antics juvenile and hisses at him when he wants to play chase around the garden. Mabel will sit quietly on my lap for hours as I read on the Sabbath – the day of rest. Nigel jumps on and off Jeremy's chair, purring loudly and begging for attention. They have such totally different characters. Mabel shies away from our visitors and Nigel plonks himself in the thick of the action. Children frequently ask me, 'Which is your favourite cat?' I really don't know. I love them both.

On winter evenings as I sit in my armchair and daydream by the fire, I imagine myself entering a benign old age surrounded by at least three of four cats. Sadly, Jeremy does not share my plans!

CHAPTER NINE –
THE BUZZ OF SUMMER

During the summer months from Shavuot in June until Rosh Hashanah, the Jewish New Year celebrated in September, there are no festivals in the calendar. There is, however, a three week period of sadness leading to Tisha B'av – the 9th day of the Hebrew month of Av. These 21 days begin with a dawn to dusk fast on the 17th day of the Hebrew month of Tammuz when no food or drink can be consumed. This Fast of Tammuz commemorates the breaching of the walls of Jerusalem which preceded the destruction of the First Temple by Nebuchadnezzar in 586 B.C.E and then the Second Temple by Titus in 70 C.E.

The time between the 17th of Tammuz and the 9th of Av is a period of mourning and no weddings are held in synagogues and religious Jews do not attend or make parties during this time. Observant Jews often wait to take their summer holidays until after the fast of Tisha B'Av when the mourning period has ended.

In addition to the destruction of both Temples on the 9th of Av there are several more tragedies that occurred on this date. The first is the expulsion of the Jews from England in 1290 which I will refer to later. The second is the expulsion of the Jews from Spain in 1492 when every Jew had to leave the country by the 9th of Av. Then, following the assassination of Archduke Ferdinand, Austro-Hungary declared war on Serbia and 4 days later on the 1st August, the Hebrew date of the 9th of Av, Germany declared war on Russia marking the third tragedy with the start of the first World War. Some historians see the arc of the Second World War as beginning with World War I and ultimately this led to the Holocaust and the destruction of 6,000,000 Jews by the Nazis.

On the night of 9th of Av we dress in sober, mourning clothes, do not wear leather shoes, we sit on the floor in the synagogue under dimmed lights and listen to the reading of the book of Eichah –

Lamentations. When we leave the synagogue we do so quietly without any farewells and we return to our homes to fast and contemplate and remember all those who died not only in the Holocaust but throughout a history of travail and persecutions and expulsions. No wonder we are called the wandering Jews and always yearned for a homeland.

In spite of the weight of sadness in the three weeks we continue to live our daily lives. At The Gables much of our time during this period is spent harvesting crops and working in the fruit and vegetable garden. Our oversized plot combines a series of raised beds, two polytunnels and some open areas for growing potatoes, root vegetables, leeks, carrots, parsnips, kale and chard, beans, artichokes and rhubarb. There are rows of blackcurrant bushes, white, red and pink currants, strawberries, raspberries and gooseberries. Many of these quintessentially English fruits were readily available in greengrocers and on market stalls when I was a child in the 1960's. Now I rarely see them in the shops and when they appear the cost is exorbitant. When younger people visit, including our 40-year-old daughter, most of them have never even seen or tasted a gooseberry. Some guess, incorrectly, that they are an oversized grape. Others look warily at the hairy green globe until they pop one in their mouth and experience a delicious taste explosion that they have never before encountered. They all want more.

It is a great treat to have so much fruit to eat fresh, to freeze or to pick for jam making. By the end of the summer the kitchen shelves are full of jars of preserves. Some of our favourites are redcurrant and onion chutney, cucumber relish, pickled beetroots, bottled blackcurrants and strawberry jam. Strings of garlics and onions are plaited later in the season and stored in the onion barn and supply our kitchen until the following spring.

The summer is also a time when new plans take shape and a few years ago Jeremy announced that he had always wanted to keep bees. Although we had been married for more than four decades I did not know that he harboured this secret wish. I tried hard to embrace his new hobby and we signed up together for beekeeping beginner classes held once a week in Moggerhanger village hall run by the Bedfordshire Beekeepers Association. I can't say that I was enthusiastic but I showed willing although not much aptitude.

Although I went along to all the lessons I realised that Jeremy's new passion was not for me. The thought of being surrounded by thousands of buzzing insects filled me with dread and not wonder. Jeremy found himself a mentor, a farmer who had kept bees for over 70 years, and they met up once a week to inspect the farmer's hives. He taught Jeremy about the bee cycle and what needed to be done and when. Our bookshelves filled with bee books and soon after lockdown the first hives arrived at The Gables and were sited in the vineyard at the far end of the vegetable garden. Jeremy ordered a colony of bees from a couple in Cheshunt who were selling them to raise money for charity and they were delivered to the smallholding. Our friend Kate had once kept a number of hives and she lent me her sting-proof jacket, hat, gloves and trousers. Throughout the spring and summer months I reluctantly helped Jeremy by puffing the smoker to keep the colony quiet during their weekly inspection. I never got used to the insects flying around my head even though it was safely ensconced in a beekeeper's veil.

Although I wasn't a natural friend to the bees I was interested in the story of beekeeping and often leafed through some of the books in the sitting room. The history was fascinating to me, the practice of the craft was not.

Cave drawings in Spain indicate that humans were practising some form of honey gathering 7,000 years ago. In more recent times, until the revolution in beekeeping in 1851, most apiarists would capture a swarm and then place them in a specially-woven type of straw basket called a skep. In order to extract the honey the keeper would have to either drive the bees out of the skep or more usually just kill them to get to the harvest. During the 18th and 19th century skeps began to be modified with Queen-excluders used in some baskets which allowed honey harvesting to take place without destroying or disturbing the entire colony.

In 1851 the Reverend Lorenzo Langstroth, an American apiarist, clergyman and teacher created the Langstroth hive which revolutionised the industry by using bee space in his top opening hive. By utitilising this area between the top of the frames and the flat coverboard above it the keeper could easily open the box where the bees were storing their honey. He later used the bee space discovery to make the frames themselves removable. His 1853 book, 'The Hive and the Honey Bee' is still in print today and Jeremy has a paperback copy on his bookshelf.

Langstroth is know as the 'Father of American beekeeping' and his design is the model for many hives that are used today. The ones that Jeremy purchased to house his bees are 'Nationals Bee Hives' which only differ slightly in dimension from the Langstroth hive.

Once the hives were in situ and the occupants were settled Jeremy was beginning to think of acquiring a second colony. Then, by chance, one Sunday morning Kate called in great excitement.

'I've just been walking the dog and I came across a swarm in the hedge a couple of fields away. You should go and collect it. Right away.'

It was July and we decided to ignore the 17th Century bee keeper's proverbial saying,

'A swarm in May is worth a load of hay,

A swarm in June is worth a silver spoon

But a swarm in July is not worth a fly.'

The bigger problem was working out how on earth we could 'collect' a swarm of bees? I remembered Heather telling me that her father, an avid apiarist, used to drive the children around the county collecting swarms which he put into cardboard boxes. Heather would sit in the back of the car, cradling a box of bees and she assured me, 'I never got stung.' With her words ringing in my ears we put on our protective suits and Jeremy and I wheeled a barrow, a box, a broom and a towel across two fields to the hedge where we found a cone of bees hanging from a branch. The insects, thousands of them, were all clustered together around their queen as if they were one entity. The structure emitted a loud and ominous buzzing and I was terrified even though Jeremy had assured me that swarming bees are not inclined to sting. Having got this far there was no turning back. Jeremy called out instructions,

'Just open the box and stand back.'

He lifted the broom up to the hedge and began to sweep downwards pushing the cone of bees towards the open box. Thousands of them dropped inside but not every one was captured and those that escaped were flying angrily around us.

'What do we do now?'

'I'm going to put the lid on and cover the box with a towel and then lift it into the wheelbarrow. You take the broom and start walking ahead of me.'

We retraced our steps in the heavy heat of July with a barrow full of bees and a stream of those left behind trying to follow. It was a long walk home as we trundled back across the fields. Kate stood at her gate and waved as we passed, pleased to see that we had followed her order to collect the free swarm. At The Gables our son and two youngest grandchildren, on their weekly Sunday visit, were eagerly waiting to welcome us home.

'Keep the children away from us,' I bellowed to my son, 'We don't want anyone to get stung.'

They all stood at a respectful distance as we continued our procession down the garden and into the vineyard where the empty hive was waiting for its new arrivals. Jeremy lifted the cover board from the top of the hive, opened the box and tipped the bees in as best he could. We were hot and sweaty and tired and both of us were dying for a cold drink.

The grandchildren were delighted to have been around when this latest adventure took place. and when we finally took off our protective clothes we all sat down and had ice lollies around the wrought-iron table in the front garden. It was mission accomplished – or so we thought as we congratulated ourselves on acquiring a 'free' colony.

Jeremy had read that we needed to let the bees settle in their new home and he patiently waited until the following morning before he went to make an inspection. When he returned from the vineyard he was ashen faced.

'There isn't a single bee in the hive. They must have swarmed again.'

I insisted on walking back with him to check the facts and as we passed the fruit bushes we spied an elegant cone of bees hanging from a blackcurrant bush right next to the path. The critters hadn't gone far.

'Thank goodness for that.'

My joy was short lived as I realized what this might mean.

'Yes, that's marvellous. Come on, back to the house we have to put our suits on again and grab the box, towel, broom and wheelbarrow.'

The whole process was repeated only this time it was just a short walk and the sun was hidden behind a bank of clouds. The bees were tipped back into the hive where they decided to set up home for good.

Our exertions were more than rewarded. At the end of the summer those free bees had produced 40 jars of clear, golden honey which we extracted with our new toy, a stainless steel drum spinner that required the application of good old fashioned manual elbow grease. It was a fine reward and a perfect start to the Jewish New Year.

CHAPTER TEN –
NEW BEGINNINGS, APPLES AND PRAYERS

Late summer and autumn are busy times at The Gables. There always seem to be several jobs to do at once even as the days begin to shorten. We inherited a number of well-established fruit trees, a Bramley apple, a Conference pear and a Victoria plum, all of which produce hundreds of pounds of fruit. Each year we planted and continue to plant more trees including cherry, pear, apple, apricot, almond, peach and nectarine. The plums are harvested in August, then the Williams pears at the end of the month and the Conference pears later in September. These have to be used or stored before they become overripe. Unblemished apples are wrapped in paper and kept on trays in a cool place and remain edible until the end of the year. The plums make excellent jam and the high level of acidity in the fruit helps it to set easily without adding pectin. Pears don't store well and I bottle them in syrup, make frozen pear sorbet and eat them straight from the tree. Cherries are stoned and stewed with blackcurrants and berries to make red and purple compotes which we keep in the freezer and defrost in the depths of winter to remind us of warm, summer days.

There are beans to dry, butternut squashes and pumpkins to hang in nets in the onion barn where they remain until we want to cook them later in winter time. Then there is cider making.

I bought Jeremy an apple press for his birthday a few years ago and it sat in a cupboard, unused, until a glut of apples and pears encouraged him to put the contraption together and bolt it to a table in the courtyard.

'Right,' he announced 'I want to fill the wheelbarrows. Will you help me? I want one barrow full of apples and the other full of pears.'

'What's the plan?' I think I knew but we hadn't really discussed this yet.

'We're going to try our hand at making cider and perry and when we've done that I'm going to use some of the honey to make mead.'

As always a new project requires more equipment. This time we had to purchase glass demijohns and funnels, cork bungs, siphoning tubes, airlocks and yeast tablets. We spent two afternoons cutting and then pulping the fruit in the press. The jars went onto a shelf in the onion barn and bubbled away until the contents stopped fermenting and then the liquid was siphoned off into clean jars and left again. Finally, some months later it was poured into dozens of empty and meticulously cleaned old whisky bottles and the new Gables alcohol was offered to our friends when we held our next big get-together. Most pronounced it, 'Surprisingly drinkable,' although, Daisy said, 'I definitely prefer your sloe gin.' It was quite pokey and potent and as time has gone on the cider, perry and especially the mead has matured and become even tastier.

Even though we are occupied with garden and orchard harvests in late August this is also a time when we are preparing spiritually for the month of High Holy Days in September and October.

The first of these major festivals is Rosh Hashanah, the Jewish New Year. During the slight easing of restrictions during Covid in 2020 we were able to find a way of celebrating this two day event with a group of men and women at The Gables using social distancing. We set out dining tables of six in the barn and each person sat in their same seat for every meal. Jeremy and I served the food with masks on our faces and gloves on our hands. The doors and windows in the house remained open all day and the weather was kind, allowing those who wished to sit outside the opportunity to pray and sing in the open air. It was an extraordinary celebration in extraordinary times. Some of the very people who doubted that we would be able to live a Jewish life in the countryside were now amongst those who joined us for the New Year services in our Gables synagogue.

The New Year is a festival which is as serious as it is joyous. It is a time to reflect on the old year and our failings whilst asking the Good Lord to grant us health and peace, prosperity and happiness and to, 'write us into the Book of Life,' for the next twelve months. In London the synagogues are usually packed with worshippers, many of whom might not step inside the building from one New Year to the next. In the time of Covid all worship in synagogues, churches and mosques was forbidden and The Gables was one of the few places where abundant space both inside and outside allowed for a small congregation to gather in the form of a hospitality setting. Each guest had to fill in a form with their name, address, contact details, and a negative Covid test at the beginning of the three days and then they were issued with an invoice for their stay at The Pop-Up Gables Guest House. We contravened none of the rules and we prayed with a greater intensity and an awareness of the natural world than perhaps we had ever done before and with renewed gratitude for our survival.

As with all our festivals, symbolic foods accompany the meals and on Rosh Hashanah it is traditional to eat honey cake and to dip apples in honey and make a bracha – a blessing – to be granted a sweet New Year. With plenty of our own apples and many jars of Gables honey it was our pleasure to be able to send gifts of both to friends and family in London and to enjoy the rest at our own table with our guests.

Jeremy was soon expanding his bee plans and he bought and set up three more hives. I was not very pleased with his new venture. The truth is that even in a full body suit I am afraid of the bees and always scared that one will get inside my hat and sting me. I only help Jeremy with the hives when it is absolutely necessary and rarely will I lift the frames that are covered in thousands of bees and often dripping in honey. Nevertheless, I am truly grateful for the sweet offerings from the hives and mindful that one bee, in its lifetime, will only make a twelfth of a teaspoon of honey. It is a precious gift.

Our beehives stood in the vineyard at the very far end of the long vegetable garden, just past the strawberry polytunnel and next to the natural pond on which live our flock of large, white Embden geese. It seemed to be the perfect location until I discovered that bees are attracted not only to flowers and blossom but also to perfume such as shampoo or even deodorants. Whenever I was weeding down near the vineyard I was the target of unprovoked attacks and if I wanted to garden I had to wear a protective suit. The situation deteriorated and one day as I was walking down to the polytunnel wearing shorts and a t-shirt a bee came straight for me. I ran as fast as I could up the garden path screaming so loudly and emitting such profanities that by the time I reached the house my neighbour Paul and his gardener (who had alerted him to the commotion) had arrived on the doorstep believing that either I was being attacked by a stranger or possibly Jeremy!

'Are you sure that you're really OK?'

'Really I am, I was just running away from a bee.'

Paul and Tracy looked at each other and raised their eyebrows. I suddenly realised how ridiculous and implausible my explanation sounded.

'Truly, I'm fine I'm just terrified of bees and I really didn't want to get stung.'

At that moment Jeremy arrived, laughing at me and surprised to see that we had visitors.

'Come in and have a cuppa. Did you really hear Gill from across the road?'

'Yes. Tracy was out in the garden and she crossed over to your gate and called out but nobody answered so she came to fetch me because she thought there might something terrible going on.'

After a cup of tea, a chocolate chip cookie and quite a lot of laughter at my expense, Paul and Tracy left with a jar of honey each to thank them for their concern and good neighbourliness.

'You have got to promise me that you will move those hives before next year. I can't go through that again.'

'I'll do it in the winter. Honest.' He rolled his eyes and sighed.

During the winter months activity in the bee hives slows right down. Their numbers reduce from about 75,000 bees in a hive to 15,000. It is a hibernation of sorts when the bees hunker down, huddle together to keep warm and feed on the stores of honey that remain in the brood box. One Thursday morning Jeremy and Chris donned two bee suits, closed up the entrances to the beehives with wooden blocks and put straps around the hives to secure them. Then they hoisted them onto wheelbarrows and moved the beehives to a different piece of ground in a patch of tall grass next to some apple trees and adjacent to the road. I was delighted.

Ten days later on the Sabbath we took our usual weekly walk around the smallholding. It was a chance to take a look at all parts of the field, the flower beds, the animals, the bees hives and an opportunity to cast an eye over all of the five-acre holding. When we arrived at the corner where the beehives stood Jeremy stopped and looked very troubled. 'Gill how many beehives can you see?'

I looked at the hives and said, 'Obviously two.'

He frowned, 'There should be four.'

'Are you certain?'

'Of course I'm certain. There are two with bees and two empty ones ready to colonise. Somebody has stolen two of our hives.'

If a person can be more than upset, Jeremy was that person. Beekeeping is an art and a passion and Jeremy had spent two years learning to keep bees and then two years looking after his hives and feeding his bees with sugar solution, checking the frames and treating them against disease. He sat in his chair for the rest of the day wondering how or why someone would steal beehives. Was it 'to order' or was it an opportunist thief who had spied the hives from the road. Either way he said, 'How on earth do you steal hives without the bees attacking. It beggars belief.' He continued to shake his head, close to tears.

'I think we should move the hives tonight,' I said to Jeremy, 'In case they return for the other two.' We couldn't move them during the day as it was the Sabbath when no work can be carried out. As the sun went down and the stars came out we donned our bee suits, grabbed a wheelbarrow and a torch and made our way to the field. First we moved the pallets on which the hives stood and wheeled them down the side of the field to a more hidden spot. Then, as light rain began to fall we strapped the hives closed and lifted the one full of bees onto the barrow and made our way slowly and carefully down the track in the darkness. As we returned for the empty hive the heavens opened but we had to finish the job and by the time we got back into the house we were soaked to the skin, aching from our journeys but relieved that the bees were safe for the night.

Notices went out on social media in case anyone had been offered a hive and a swarm or seen anything unusual but there was no news of the bees just a lot of sympathetic messages such as, 'Who could do such a thing,' or, 'What sort of people would steal a hive full of bees,' and many that said, 'I hope the bastards got well and truly stung,' and worse.

Losses, injuries and disease are part of the territory for the smallholder and farmer. They are unavoidable but we all try our best to minimise them and at The Gables we are able to keep a close eye on our animals. The very first stock we bought were the two Dexter heifers, Lucy and Beattie, who grew into glossy coated adults. A bucket of concentrates was all that was required for the girls to follow us anywhere and whilst they were eating we could stroke their warm hides and admire them. In truth Jeremy had a greater fondness for the cows than I did and I wasn't best pleased when, in her haste to get to the feed bucket, Beattie inadvertently stepped on my little toe and broke it. It was agony to put on shoes for several weeks until the swelling went down. In time I forgave Beattie but I definitely preferred Lucy after that incident!

When both the girls were fully grown we borrowed a young bull, Milton, from our friend Kate and he came to live at The Gables for a few months and earned his keep by getting both cows in calf. Cows are pregnant for nine months and as their due dates approached we hoped that we wouldn't have to be midwives at the delivery. In the event both girls gave birth without any help from us. Lucy calved first and a couple of weeks later Beattie became a mother. The beautiful black bull calves were up on their feet within the hour and sucking from their mothers. Kate came over to see the newborns and pronounced them, 'Very fine little boys,' and we felt rather pleased with ourselves. We must have gone out to see and admire and photograph the little ones nearly every hour. Lucy and Beattie co-parented their offspring with one cow taking herself off to graze and the other keeping an eye on the babies and even licking them both. It was a great arrangement.

As I watched Larry, Lucy's calf, sucking from her udder one afternoon all seemed well with mother and son and I began to think about the phrase that Jeremy often quoted, 'More than the calf wants to suck the cow wants to give suck.' It's a line from a chapter (Pesachim 112a) in The Talmud. The Talmud is a record of rabbinic debates in the 2nd to 5th century on the teachings of the Torah, the five books of Moses known as The Old Testament. It seems that the rabbis in those ancient times were far more aware of nature and the natural world than we are in this so called 'modern and enlightened' age.

Although we have been vegetarians all our married life and brought up our son and daughter in the same way, with our grandson following in his mother's footsteps, we still ate dairy produce and, as of today, we still eat some cheese and milk and butter each week. Cheese is one of my favourite foods and although I gave it up for a month at the start of 2023 I backslid and started again but in smaller quantities. I found it easier to stop smoking than to stop eating cheese. I am wracked with guilt about this especially when I see my vegan nephew who sticks religiously to a non-dairy diet. I don't know if he does this for health or ethical reasons but I certainly want to try and stop simply because I now know that dairy production is cruel.

Having watched our cows give birth and suckle their calves for many months I realise that the bond between calf and mother is strong and powerful as nature intended. The calf is created to drink milk from its mother's udder just as human babies are born to suck milk from their mother's breast. In almost every milking herd of cows in this country, and in all developed parts of the world, the newborn calf must be torn away from its mother in order that the milk she produces can be mechanically released and sent away to be processed into pasteurised milk and butter and made into cheese for humans to consume. The cow looks constantly for her missing infant and the calf is either shot or otherwise disposed of within a matter of days or fed mechanically on milk replacer. This is cruel beyond imagining and some recent documentaries have been aired on television which show in graphic detail the agony of the mother and the bewilderment of the calf. There are many more films that can be seen on Youtube and on animal welfare charity sites. All of them make for difficult and distressing viewing.

I have made a search for ethical dairies in the UK. They are few and far between. The Ethical Dairy in Rainton, Scotland directed me to a website, Cowcalfdairies.co.uk which lists less than a dozen farms where cows are allowed to keep their calves at foot for at least six months. The farmer milks the cows just once and day and the rest of the time the calf may drink from its mother. The commercial milk yield is reduced and the price of this ethical product, including cheese, butter and ice cream, is higher than milk and dairy products available from a conventional herd but for all concerned the result is a contented cow, calf and customers.

At The Gables we practice ethical dairying. We allow the goat kids to stay with their mothers until they are weaned. Only then do we take all the milk for our own kitchen where Jeremy is beginning to make a variety of soft and hard cheeses including ricotta, feta, mozzarella, wensleydale and cheddar.

More and more super farms are being set up in this country along the lines of those animal factories found all over the United States of America and beyond. In April 2023 one of these American cattle prison camps exploded, killing 18,000 animals probably due to faulty electrical equipment setting light to the methane produced by the cattle. There are reportedly many such accidents including pigs and chickens kept in similarly confined and overcrowded and unnatural conditions. The cattle never see a blade of grass or run free. They live on hard surfaces and eat a diet of soya and cereals that will fatten them as quickly as possible to provide meat for human consumption.

In Britain, which has always prided itself on high animal welfare standards, there are now over 1,000 livestock megafarms and some hold more than 1,000,000 birds. Of these three quarters house poultry, 200 are for pigs and there are at least 19 dairies where cows are zero grazed and permanently housed inside sheds. The largest of these cattle farms holds 2,000 animals.

Anyone who works with animals, or lives alongside them or cares to find out about rearing livestock will realise that this is so far removed from the natural world as to reduce these creatures to commodities raised solely to provide cheap meat, eggs and milk for us, the human consumer. Those working in such places will quickly need to become desensitised to the welfare and emotions of these sentient creatures. It is quite simply horrific and we need to do something about this for the sake of our own humanity, for the sake of the planet and above all for the sake of all those animals bred into a life of captivity, humiliation and cruelty with absolutely no means of escape. I know that I must take that step again of giving up dairy foods until we can make enough cheese to satisfy my dairy cravings.

We raise animals and, as I delight in telling all our male visitors, one only needs a single ram, bull, billy goat or cockerel in each group of females. The rest must go into the food chain but not until they have reached maturity, lived a good while in natural surroundings and been lovingly raised by us and the family. That is the reality of keeping livestock but that doesn't mean that we should kill and eat animals or their produce without having any awareness of how they are raised and killed. In the book of Genesis, in the story of Creation, God gives Adam dominion over the animals but he does not say that he can be cruel to them and treat them as he wants. Maybe that is why there are so many dietary laws in the Old Testament, to make us aware of where our food comes from and that we should care for our animals in a way that encourages us to be better, more sensitive and kind individuals. That, sadly, in modern day orthodox Judaism is rarely acknowledged and it is a painful fact for me to own. There are tiny shoots of change amongst some of the younger generation of Jews but these are generally people who are more liberal in their Jewish practices and amongst the traditionally orthodox as in the wider non-Jewish population they mostly neither care, nor are aware of how their meat and poultry and fish is farmed and raised and placed on their dinner plates.

Lucy and Beattie were a great source of joy at The Gables and also an educational tool. One Boxing Day morning our seven-year-old grandson was upstairs in the bedroom when he called me.

'Grandma come up here. I think Beattie is having a baby.'

The little fella was absolutely right. Beattie was standing in the paddock near the climbing frame having wandered away from her stable mate Lucy. Cows and sheep and goats usually separate themselves from the flock or herd when they are about to deliver. A bit of privacy is appreciated by labouring human females too and we were used to this separation as a sign of impending birth.

'Look grandma, there's a pink balloon coming out of Beattie's bottom.'

'It's the sack that the baby is in. Let's keep watching.' Within seconds the calf's head and front legs appeared in a diving position pointing towards the ground and after one big push from Beattie the calf slithered onto the grass followed, a few minutes later, by the afterbirth. It was a textbook delivery.

We gave mother and baby half an hour to bond before we disturbed them and then went to see the newborn to admire the latest arrival.

A few weeks earlier our grandson and a friend had arranged to come to The Gables for a day trip and I collected them both in my car in London and drove up the A1 with the boys chatting away on the back seats. The talk turned to the animals that they would see at the smallholding and grandson described the cows and the sheep, the chickens, ducks and geese that his pal would meet. Then grandson fell silent. He must have remembered when, on a previous visit in the spring, we had rented a Dexter bull who came to stay with the girls to get them in calf. Jeremy, grandson and I had watched as the large, red bull with the typical ring through his nose, was disgorged from the farmer's trailer. The bull shook his bulky head and lumbered over to the cows. Within a minute the huge fellow had singled out red-headed Lucy and jumped on top of her. She collapsed under his weight. We were shocked. We shouldn't have worried because Lucy worked it all out. She went and stood against the barn wall and when Adnams mounted her again she was able to use the wall to support her and it was mission accomplished. None of us could forget such a sight.

As I drove the boys towards the smallholding I caught grandson saying to his seven year old friend,

'If you see a cow and a bull and you think that they're fighting they're not. They're......' and here, thankfully, our grandson ran out of the vocabulary to continue the sex education lesson. This was just as well because both boys attended an orthodox Jewish primary school and I was sure that neither the parents of grandson's companion nor his teachers would have appreciated this ad hoc introduction to the facts of life.

Bedfordshire, where we live, is a low risk area for bovine tuberculosis (TB). The cows, by law, have to be tested by a vet every four years and on September 4th 2018 Lucy and Beattie were expecting a visit from a ministry-approved vet. On that day two areas of hair on the cows' necks were shaved and then injected, one with bovine tuberculin and the second with avian tuberculin. Four days after the injections the vet returned to measure any reaction to the substance. The rules are that if a cow reacts visibly and measurably more to the bovine than the avian tuberculin the cow is considered to be a reactor and subject to movement restrictions.

To our surprise, disappointment and consternation Beattie had a reaction and a raised temperature whereas Lucy did not. However, apart from being unable to move the girls off the premises and answering questions as to which other cows ours had been in contact with, we were not unduly concerned. A second test was carried out and we expected this to be negative, revealing the first results to be a not uncommon false positive.

We were devastated when the vet returned four days after the second test, examined Beattie and turned to us with a sympathetic expression. 'I am so sorry to have to tell you that Beattie has a positive reaction again and she will have to be isolated from Lucy. Our office will arrange a removal date within sixty days to come and collect her.'

'But,' pleaded Jeremy, 'She's pregnant. She's never been away from The Gables and she and Lucy have been together all their lives. How is it possible for one of them to have TB and not the other? She's never coughed or shown any signs of being anything other than healthy.'

'Look,' said the vet, 'It's an old test and it sometimes throws up a false positive but the law requires that any reactor animal is destroyed. We will do a post mortem and send you the results. She may well have lesions in her lungs that you wouldn't be able to see. Oh, and you will be notified of compensation.'

We had no recourse to an appeal. It was decreed by law and we awaited the call from the transport department giving us the date of removal. We were shocked and sad and we also grieved for Lucy who was no longer allowed to live with her stablemate. They could see each other across the field and I'm sure they couldn't understand why they had been separated. Lucy would have to be tested 60 days later and then a further 60 days after that to establish whether she had contracted the disease. She tested negative both times.

Within a fortnight Beattie had been loaded onto a trailer. We stroked her and said, 'Goodbye,' feeling like traitors sending her to an untimely and unnecessary death trying to console ourselves with the knowledge that Beattie had lived a wonderful life for five years, given birth to two calves and suckled each for a year after their births. As I wrote in my blog on September 9th 2018, *'Beattie has been cosseted and overfed with sweet hay, fresh pasture, buckets of concentrates and plenty of greens and windfall apples from the garden and the orchard.'*

Indoors, at his desk, Jeremy continued to research TB tests with a growing sense of injustice and scepticism which was compounded ten days after Beattie's destruction when the results of the post mortem revealed there were no visible lesions on her lungs. Then, as if to bribe us for the unnecessary destruction of our cow, we received a cheque in the sum of £1,200, nearly four times the amount that we had originally paid for her. When my brother asked what had happened to Beattie I told him with a mixture of black humour and anger, 'I think I'll buy some more pedigree cows and infect them with TB and I'll make a fortune.' Something seemed wrong with the test, the lack of appeal and the outrageously inflated compensation.

Lucy was now on her own, retested and shown to be TB-free, and pregnant. Kate kindly lent us Bella to keep Lucy company until Lucy calved on February 28th 2019. Bella was Beattie's last calf who had grown into a beautiful cow and we had sold her to Kate as we did not have enough acreage to feed three cattle. Bella was pregnant with her own first calf and she remained at the Gables until, on a sunny April morning Bella went into labour when I was home alone. She was struggling and straining and her tail was lifting up and down, a sure sign of impending parturition. Kate was away visiting her daughter and Jeremy was in London working and I was sure that I wouldn't be able to help a labouring cow on my ownsome. I picked up the phone and called Phil who helps Kate on her smallholding. Thankfully he was driving over to see some livestock a few miles away and he turned his car around and hotfooted it back to The Gables to lend his expertise.

'Have you got some rubber gloves?'

I kept a box of them in the kitchen and ran inside to grab them. Phil put on the gloves and he put his hands up the backside of Bella to feel for the calf's nose and try to find out if the calf would get through the first-time mother's narrow passageway.

'I think she'll be OK but she might need some help.'

Phil pulled at the delivery end as I stood beside Bella at her head end whispering to her and trying to encourage her to push. The calf was a tight fit but within 15 minutes he emerged, perfect and slick with mucus which Phil drew away from his nose and mouth so that he could breathe.

'Wow. Well done, I don't know if she could have done it without you.'

'Oh, she just needed a little bit of help,' Phil said modestly.

Bella attended dutifully to her offspring, licking and nuzzling him and very soon the bull calf was up on his feet and sucking at Bella's udder. Once Phil had seen the calf feeding he peeled of his gloves, washed his hands under the outside tap and got back in his car and was on his way.

The next day, when Kate returned, she drove over with her trailer and she and Phil loaded Bella and calf onto the vehicle and drove them back across the road to join the rest of Kate's herd.

Red-headed Lucy, who had given birth to a black girl calf, Lilly, two months before Bella was now enjoying the spring and summer sunshine with her offspring. I wondered if Lucy still thought about her old friend Beattie.

By the time that we went into Lockdown in March 2020 Lilly was fully grown and she and mother Lucy were living at The Gables alongside 14 sheep, 20 lambs and assorted poultry and geese. The weather was gloriously hot and dry and very soon the grass stopped growing and we needed to give the livestock hay to supplement the diminishing supply of pasture. There was no sign of rain and we were beginning to wonder what to do when two friends in the village came to see us (outdoors of course). They saw the state of our yellowing field and the husband said, 'Why don't you move Lucy and Lilly to our place. We have a field full of grass and wildflowers that hasn't been grazed for a couple of years. It would be fun to have some animals around the place.' Be careful what you wish for!

When we told Kate about their kind offer she asked us if she could bring her little bull, Sammi, to the field with our girls and our friends agreed. That solved the problem of getting the cows to the village because we didn't own a cattle trailer but Kate does. The next morning Jeremy, Kate and I and our grandson walked around the new field to check the state of the fences and hedges and we made some minor repairs with wooden stakes and wire and hoped that would keep the cattle inside the field, off the road and out of our friends' garden. That afternoon we loaded the three animals onto Kate's trailer and drove them to the village, up the driveway of the house and in through the metal gate leading to the field. The animals went running off hither and thither, enjoying the taste of juicy pasture and eager to explore their new surroundings. All seemed well but the next morning, before we had time to go and check on the cattle, we received a telephone call.

'The cows are on our lawn. You better come right away and get them back into the field.' Our friend didn't sound too pleased. I couldn't blame him as they have a beautifully landscaped garden and pond and they hadn't signed up to the grass being decorated with large cow pats. The three of us rushed down to the village with more stakes and wire and plenty of tempting food and three buckets. Luckily Lucy and Lilly were used to coming to us when they heard the rattle of the feed bowls and the bull calf, Sammi, followed on their heels. Then we set about repairing the damage to the fencing as best we could and set up a twice-daily rota for checking on the stock.

All went well for a week or two and then Kate asked our friends if she could move, 'Two cows and their two calves as I'm a bit low on pasture. In return I'll give you some beef when they go for slaughter.' The deal was done.

Now there were seven cattle in the field and more chances of trouble and mischief. When another breakout occurred I had a serious talk with Jeremy.

'I'm fed up with going to the village twice a day to check on cows.'

'You don't have to go. We all take it in turns,' he countered.

'But I only want to keep animals at The Gables where we can see them all the time. It's a pain and a bind to have to drive up and down every day.'

I literally stamped my foot.

'I absolutely insist that we sell the cows.' Jeremy reluctantly agreed and put an advert on an animal website and within a few days we were showing the girls to potential buyers from near and far. Lucy and Lilly had been running with Sammi, an uncastrated young bull, and there was every possibility that one or both of the girls could be pregnant. We told prospective purchasers that they might be lucky and get more than just two cows but we weren't giving any guarantees. In the event a local young couple made an offer for the girls and one sunny July afternoon Kate brought up a collection of metal hurdles to the field and with the inducement of food we all managed to corral the cows inside the makeshift pen and then load them onto the farmer's trailer. It was a bittersweet farewell and marked the end of our cow-keeping days at The Gables. The farmer's wife said, 'Feel free to come and visit them whenever you want. We're only a mile down the road.' We didn't go and see them but we got an email to let us know that they had settled in well and nine months later, in April 2021, the farmer's wife contacted us to let us know that Lilly and Lucy had both given birth to healthy calves. 'Please do come and see them if you'd like.' A date and time was arranged and on the day we drove up into the yard where 'our girls' and their calves were standing with three other cows outside a barn and next to a feeder full of hay. Before we had even opened the car doors Lucy and Lilly were bellowing and when we stood by the fence Lucy raced over to me and stuck my outstretched hand inside her mouth and sucked on it again and again. The farmer's wife said, 'Honestly, they only started kicking off when you drove up. They've never done that before. They must remember you.'

'Lilly, Lucy, you clever girls. I'm so proud of you,' I cooed at them

There is absolutely no doubt that the girls knew us, remembered us and wanted to greet us. Cows have memories and they deserve to be treated with kindness, care and compassion. We missed them but it was time to move on and soon we had other animals taking their place.

CHAPTER ELEVEN – GOATS AND ANTISEMITISM

The High Holy Days of the Jewish calendar extend from Rosh Hashanah, the two-day Jewish New Year up to and including the most solemn day of the year, Yom Kippur – the Day of Atonement. These ten days are called the Days of Awe and certain prayers are inserted into the daily services when we ask the Good Lord to judge us favourably because on Yom Kippur we believe that our fate will be sealed for the following year. In the month leading up to the 25 hours of fasting on the Day of Atonement we are obliged to ask for pardon from friends and family if we have hurt or offended them and, having made our peace, we then ask forgiveness from the Lord for sins we may have consciously or inadvertently committed in those 12 months. Many less observant Jews will fast on Yom Kippur and attend prayer services even though they might not do so throughout the rest of the year.

We used to go to London for the High Holy Days but since the first Covid lockdown we have organised groups of friends and family to stay, pray, eat and then observe the fast with us. We warned our neighbours that they might hear singing from The Gables and even the loud blowing of the shofar – the ram's horn trumpet – which sounds 100 notes during both days of Rosh Hashanah and a final long note after the closing prayers on Yom Kippur.

Our Jacob ram, Tufty, has a magnificent pair of curly horns that would make two fantastic trumpets but the proprietors of the abattoirs do not want to go to the trouble of returning horns from slaughtered animals. We hope that Tufty will have many more healthy and productive years at The Gables but when his time is nigh we will see whether we can persuade his dispatchers to save his horns and maybe, one day, we will blow the notes on the High Holy Days, remembering his good nature and good service.

One of the central features of the Yom Kippur service (which commences at sunset and finishes 25 hours later) is the description of the ritual slaughter of two goats whose fate was drawn by lots at the hand of the High Priest of the Temple in Jerusalem, in biblical times. One goat was to be sacrificed on the altar of the Temple and the other was to be taken to the wilderness and thrown off a cliff bearing the sins of the nation. In 1530 a Protestant scholar, William Tyndale, translated the Hebrew Bible into English and when he came upon the passages describing the Yom Kippur goats he mistakenly thought that the animal designated for Azazel was set free to wander in the wilderness. Tyndale called this creature the escape goat which in time became scapegoat, a term which is still in use today meaning someone blamed for the misdeeds of others. Jewish communities, like many other minorities throughout the world, have often found themselves scapegoated down the centuries.

Four years after we moved to Bedfordshire Jeremy began to think of getting a pair of goats for The Gables. When we lived in Devon at the Old Forge, over 40 years ago, we owned and milked two large, white Saanen goats called Penelope and Prudence. They had long horns, evil, slitty eyes and they gave me a hard time when I was called upon to milk them. As far as they were concerned Jeremy was their King Billy and they stood quietly when he took them to the milking shed. If Jeremy was at college or busy in the garden I took my turn with the goats. They delighted in putting their hooves in the bucket or kicking it over, looking at me as if to say, 'You can't tell us what to do. Only Jeremy can do that.' They were also accomplished escape artists and so we had to tether them in the field with very long chains which allowed them to graze in a large circle without jumping over or burrowing through the hedges. If we stayed in bed later than usual we would hear the goats banging on the wooden shed door chiding us for daring to have a lie in. We sold milk from the house to locals who were allergic to cows' milk. Back in the 1970's supermarkets didn't stock goats' milk and we had a number of regular customers who came to see us once a week to collect their supplies.

This time, at The Gables, we were looking for a small breed that produced only a litre or so of milk a day. We had no plans to sell the milk but we did want to try our hands at cheesemaking. The Golden Guernsey goat fitted the bill but, being rare and sought after, they were not readily available to buy. These goats nearly became extinct during the Second World War when the Germans invaded the Channel Islands and requisitioned most of the livestock. A Miss Miriam Milbourne hid her prized Golden Guernsey goats at great personal risk and, at the end of the war, these 30 animals became the goats from which all future stock was bred. I believe that we owe Miss Milbourne a great debt for saving the species.

The FAO – The Food and Agricultural Organisation of the United Nations – puts the Golden Guernsey on their endangered species list which records only 1,500 breeding females worldwide. With so few available nanny goats it proved difficult to find Golden Guernseys to buy and for six months Jeremy tried to track some down to add to our Gables animal collective. Eventually he found a breeder in Lincolnshire who was advertising two young pedigree nannies for sale, ready for collection in November 2019. He contacted Mrs Turner straight away, agreed a price and told her that we definitely wanted the half-sisters, Willow and Wisp, and we would come to collect them at her convenience. A date a few months ahead was fixed but just two days before our trek north up the A1 we received an apologetic call from Mrs Turner. 'I'm so sorry,' she said to us both as we listened on Jeremy's speaker phone, and our hearts sank. Had she decided to sell the girls to a higher bidder? She continued, 'Willow must have reached 'maturity' early and her father caught the smell and before I could stop him he had jumped over two fences and I think he has done the deed. I am very much afraid that Willow is pregnant. It's not good for such a young goat to give birth and she'll probably have trouble kidding.' Jeremy assured Mrs Turner that we were still more than willing to buy the goats and were coming to get them as arranged. Mrs Turner continued, 'That billy was lent out to another breeder and when he came back he was in a feral state and was completely unmanageable.' By the time we drove to Lincolnshire, 48 hours later, the sentence was passed and Mr Billy had been dispatched and butchered and was sitting in Mrs Turner's freezer!

Mr and Mrs Turner's smallholding was in the heart of the countryside a few miles from the historic city of Lincoln. It seemed further than 70 miles because we were travelling in our old Land Rover

Defender, with draughty, rickety windows, hard seats, no radio and erratic heating. The top speed was 65 mph but often, on narrow and pot holed side roads, we went much more slowly. To while away the journey I used my iPhone to Google information about the towns that we passed as we headed north. It was then that I read about the medieval history of Stamford and the massacre of Jews. The blood-letting took place in 1190 in the first year of the reign of Richard I or, as he was popularly known in my childhood Ladybird book series, Richard the Lionheart. Thirty Jews were killed soon after the first Crusade to the Holy Land left these shores. I hadn't known this before our drive to Lincolnshire, nor much about the story of Little St Hugh of Lincoln and the infamous blood libel against the Jews of that city. What began as snippets of information read above the noise of the Defender on the way to buy two goats, would become a journey of discovery and research into the history of the Jews in England but before I could find out more of this story we had first to buy and then bring Willow and Wisp home to The Gables.

Mr and Mrs Turner were a delightful couple in their seventies, who had worked and lived on the land for all their married lives. They kept some sheep as well as chickens and goats and Mr Turner had been an employed shepherd in his younger days and their home was rented from the farmer.

'Hello,' said Mrs Turner. 'Let's go round the side to meet the girls and then we can come back indoors to do the necessary paperwork.'

We followed our host to a small pen next to the house where we were introduced to Willow and Wisp. Willow was the taller of the two goats and had a shaggy, white coat and an intelligent face. Wisp was smaller and coffee coloured. She was shy and hid behind her half-sister. 'They're lovely,' I said to Mrs Turner and meant it. Smaller than I had imagined, they were extremely attractive and I liked them instantly. Mr Turner joined us at the pen. He had recently had a knee replacement operation but in spite of that and his advancing years, gnarled, farmers hands and short stature he was strong and agile as he shifted metal hurdles around the paddock and pen preparing the girls for their move to the Land Rover. 'I'm glad you like them,' said Mrs Turner, 'Let's all go inside and have a cup of tea.'

We sat in their neat as a pin kitchen and I kept looking at the

GOATS AND ANTISEMITISM

freezer, standing against the kitchen wall, which I realised was the resting place of the feral Mr Billy. I couldn't help feeling sorry for him, even though he had violated his own daughter. When we were ready to leave, having filled in the paperwork and paid the bill, we led the girls out to the Land Rover. Although the kids were not fully grown they were well-built and heavy and we had to strain to lift them up from the ground into the back of the vehicle. As we turned the Land Rover around in the narrow lane, Mrs Turner stood and waved. 'I'll keep in touch and let you know how they are,' I called out of the window and with that we were on our way home with two beautiful, goats who sat quietly on the straw probably wondering where they were going. When we got back to The Gables we held onto the goats by their leads as we coaxed them into the paddock. Everything was strange and unfamiliar to them but eventually we got them into the barn where we had placed fresh hay, a layer of straw, a bucket of clean water and some tempting concentrates in a bowl. We shut them in for the night and hoped that they would settle. I emailed Mrs Turner a photograph to show her that the girls had arrived and were installed in their new home. 'Thank you, glad they got home safely,' she wrote back. 'I like the look of their shed it's much bigger than the pen they had here. Please let me know if Willow has kids.' After a long journey, and the excitement of finally buying and bringing home two Golden Guernseys we were ready for a good night's sleep. It had been quite a day.

The next morning at my desk, I consulted the internet and then started to pull out books from our Jewish library. Over the next weeks and months I bought further volumes, mainly out of print, through second hand book sites. I joined the Jewish Historical Society so that I could access their archives and attend any relevant lectures. Some months later I decided to write a book for school-age children on the medieval history of the Jews in England. I consulted our long-standing friend of over 50 years who was a prolific writer of children's non-fiction books for most of his working life. Some of his books were historical, some on more contemporary subjects (our then teenage children had thought that the one about illegal drugs was the coolest) and he gave me advice on the word count, picture placement, chapter breakdown and more. My enthusiasm for the project led me to make a pilgrimage to Stamford on a cold, sunny Thursday in February where I arrived in time to attend a communion service at one of the town's five medieval churches.

Stamford is a strikingly pretty town with a population of 20,000 featuring many 17th and 18th century buildings. It is frequently used for film and television locations. Jeremy and I had visited the area some years earlier, on a warm June day, with two Israeli friends who were staying at The Gables. We had purchased geraniums and cut flowers from one of the market stalls and Daphna had remarked, 'What a beautiful place this is. Wouldn't it be delightful to live in such a town.' What we did not then know was that this place had such a chilling history. As my later research expanded I uncovered more about the bloody past of Stamford's Jews and the terrible trials and accusations, persecutions and murders of so many innocent Jewish men, women and children in Medieval England. It was a fascinating, terrifying and troubling story that haunts me to this day.

In 1300, there were 5000 residents of Stamford, making it quite a large town for that time and from the early 12th century there was a small Jewish community established near the castle. William of Normandy encouraged, or possibly coerced, some of his Jewish subjects to come from Rouen after 1066 and live in his newly conquered land. Others may have followed their co-religionists with a view to expanding their businesses in a new country. There was no banking system in existence and the Church forbade Christians from lending money at interest to other Christians. The Jews were literate and numerate and had already become skilled at money lending on the Continent as well as trading in gold and silver. William needed to finance an ambitious programme of castle building to secure and establish his power base in his newly conquered territory and this service was supplied by the Jews. In return King William granted them special privileges which included freedom of movement, exemption from road tolls and the right to rule themselves in their own religious courts.

The population of England at the time was just 1,500,000 people and the Jews never numbered more than 14,000 throughout the period 1066 to 1291. Only six percent of the English were literate but all the incoming Jews read and wrote, mostly French, Hebrew and some Latin and later English. Their strong links to family and businesses in France were useful to a monarch who spent much of his time travelling between the two countries.

The first Jews settled in London and Oxford and later moved on to other towns including Lincoln and Stamford. In 1100 King Henry 1 issued a charter which stated that the Jews, unlike the rest of the population, were not subject to the rule of the Ecclesiastical courts and the community became known as The King's Jews – answerable only to him and under his jurisdiction. Their education as well as their religion and close relationship to the King and his court set them apart from most of the people amongst whom they lived and may well have given rise to resentment amongst the local populations. These incomers had their own customs and religious practices, they ate different foods, they rarely drank with their neighbours and were often welcomed at court. Some of the wealthier Jews even employed Christian servants.

The fortunes of the tiny Jewish communities ebbed and flowed according to the attitude of the monarch who sat on the throne at the time. Some of the rulers were more and others less well-disposed towards the Jews but all of them needed to borrow money to finance their armies, the dowries of their children, the upkeep of their castles and the Royal Court. The King had the power to tax his Jews on any money they earned and these taxes were often heavily increased when the King's exchequer was depleted.

During the years of the Anarchy, the 19 years that followed the death of Henry 1 when Henry's daughter Matilda and Henry's nephew Stephen were fighting over the succession, the Jews abandoned trading in gold and silver as travel became dangerous in the lawless countryside. These were uncertain times for all and anger was often turned against the Jews. With the accession to the throne of Henry II stability was restored and the Jews were once again free to trade and prosper, with one money lender, Aaron of Lincoln, said to have been richer even than the King himself. One of Aaron's houses still stands today in the city of Lincoln not so many miles away from the smallholding of Mr and Mrs Turner.

When Henry died his son Richard was crowned King. His coronation at Westminster Abbey in 1189 was the occasion of a riot in London where many Jews were killed or injured and their homes burned and looted. While Christian men were sailing with King Richard to the Holy Land hoping to free Jerusalem from the infidels, the Jews in

England were perceived to be enjoying their imagined wealth in peace. Further attacks against Jewish communities took place not only in London but soon after in Lyn, Norwich, Lincoln, Colchester, Thetford and then in Stamford where on March 7th 1190, 30 Jews were killed by the mob. More terrors followed and on the 16th March in 1190 the greatest loss of Jewish life in this period took place in York at Clifford's Tower.

The Sheriff of York had left the city to join King Richard on the Third Crusade and when a fire broke out in the city on 16th March some citizens took advantage of the chaos to enter the house of a Jewish man called Benedict. The mob stole the owner's valuables and killed everyone inside. Another Jew, fearing that the same fate awaited him and others in the community, led the remaining Jewish families to the King's Tower where they sought protection from the keeper of the castle, as was their right under the Charter of Henry I. One of the ringleaders of the mob, Richard Malebisse who was believed to owe a number of debts to the Jews, then offered safe passage to any Jews who agreed to leave the Tower and convert to Christianity. Those who took that option were murdered as soon as they left the building. At the same time the rioters entered York Minster where the records of debts to Jews were kept, and destroyed the scrolls. Trapped inside the Tower with no hope of escape the families decided to commit suicide rather than face death at the hands of the mob. Each father burned his family's possessions then killed his wife and children before taking his own life. All told 150 men, women and children died on that terrible day and they are commemorated at Clifford's Tower which is, today, a historic site managed by The English Heritage Trust

Succeeding kings, John, then Henry III taxed and oppressed the Jewish community to the point of penury and when Edward I came to power in 1272 a Statute was passed forbidding Jews from money-lending. The Jews, prohibited from owning land, unable to join Christian guilds and thereby shut out of any means of earning a living, inevitably slid into poverty. No longer any financial use to the King, Edward issued an edict on July 18th 1290 expelling the entire Jewish Population and giving them until November to leave England's shores or face death. Rabbi Meir of Norwich wrote the following lines with a broken heart,

'Forced away from where we dwelt

We go like cattle to the slaughter
A slayer
Stands above us all
We burn and die.'

In just 200 years the Jews arrived in England, thrived, were systematically impoverished and then expelled. Jews were absent from England until the time of Oliver Cromwell 350 years later.

With the weight of this history on my shoulders I felt nervous as I entered the church in the centre of the town. I had read on the Stamford website that this was the only place of worship to be holding a Holy Communion service on that Thursday morning in February and I was curious. As the large, wooden door clanged shut the handful of elderly people in the huge building all turned to look at me. A priest in long white vestments was giving a sermon from a raised stone pulpit in the corner. I didn't really understand what he was saying but he kept talking about the Lamb of God. This was a concept with which I was completely unfamiliar and I resolved to ask my friend Heather what it meant. The following week when Heather and I met for our weekly walk, she explained that the Lamb refers to Jesus. She told me to look at pictures of the recently restored 15th century painting in the Cathedral of Ghent in Belgium. This depicts the Lamb on an altar, wounded and with his blood flowing into a chalice. The creature has a disturbingly human-like face with eyes that seem to look straight at the viewer. The Lamb is simultaneously an animal and also represents the man Jesus who Christians believe was sacrificed to carry away the sins of the world. At the end of the prayers several of those seated stood and processed up the long aisle to the high altar where the priest gave them a sip of wine from a large silver chalice wiping the cup after each congregant had drunk before offering it to the next. He also placed a small wafer on each person's tongue. The body and blood of Christ – that much I knew although I had thought that it was only Catholics who partook of the wine and the wafer, believing that these really do become the body and the blood of Christ, a transformation known as transubstantiation. Again, Heather put me right. The Protestant Church uses these symbols to remind their adherents of Jesus, without believing that they really turn into his flesh and blood. It seemed that I was just as ignorant of Christian practices as they probably were of Jewish rituals and prayers.

People smiled at me as they returned to their seats and we all shook each other's hands in an offering of peace greeting. After the service I remained behind. 'May I have a word please if you have a minute?' I asked the priest. He stopped and gave me a smile as I explained, 'I'm not from Stamford but I'm carrying out some research on the Jewish history of Medieval Stamford. Did you know that Jews were massacred here in 1190.' His smile disappeared and he pursed his lips and said, 'I'm sorry I really haven't got the time to talk at the moment.' He turned and walked back up the aisle and disappeared through a side door. That was it. I would get no more from him. Maybe he thought I was expecting an apology. Maybe I was. I was left standing next to the wooden pews, inwardly shaking with anger at my abrupt dismissal.

Where could I go now? It was time to move on and I zipped up my coat, opened the heavy door and began to walk in the direction of the shops, hoping to get my bearings in the town. Along the pedestrianised High Street I happened upon the library and went in. Libraries are my favourite public buildings and after my encounter in the church and my general unease with the history of the town it was a relief to feel comfortable and safe when I stepped inside. Approaching one of the librarians I asked, 'Do you by any chance have a map of the town?' He walked me over to a set of drawers, and pulled out two sheets of paper. 'This should help you.' One was headed, 'A stroll through Medieval Stamford' and the other a modern street plan. The Medieval map was just what I wanted. I set off towards the site of the castle where just a plaque and a tiny part of a wall remained. My investigations had taught me that the Jews would have lived close to the castle so that in times of civil unrest they, their families and their valuables, could be shielded inside by the Barons and Sheriffs appointed by the King. Eating my sandwiches on a bench by the remains of the castle, I felt the same sense of foreboding as I had 48 years earlier when Jeremy and I had stopped for a few hours in Munich. It was as if my brethren were calling out to me from beneath the ground, imploring me not to forget them.

In the succeeding days, after my pilgrimage, I prepared a few pages to read to our friends who were coming to The Gables in June of that year to celebrate the festival of Shavuot. After our festive lunch, our guests listened attentively as I delivered my paper. When I finished reading they asked me several questions and I felt encouraged and thought that I might turn my research into a textbook but my enthusiasm was waning. Summer is a busy time at The Gables and I really wanted to spend all the daylight hours gardening. Sitting indoors at a desk had lost its appeal. The story that began with a journey to Lincolnshire to collect two goats uncovered a familiar tale of prejudice and antisemitism that has been repeated down the ages and throughout the world and continues to this present day.

As Mrs Turner suspected, Willow was indeed pregnant and as she neared the date of delivery her udder began to bag up and her belly to swell. We were prepared for a difficult labour with a young, first-time mother. Firmly in national Lockdown we were going to have to help Willow without the assistance of a vet. Our four Covid refugees from London watched and waited as the days went by, excited at the prospect of playing with kids. Then, one May morning, we opened the goat shed and to our joy and delight Willow had kidded all by herself and given birth to a boy and girl. Their coats were soft and velvety and they had such pretty faces. The little girl was on her feet and doing well but the boy had retroverted front legs and was struggling to stand. I thought that he might be permanently disabled. Jeremy said, 'You're worrying unnecessarily he's going to be fine.' He proved to be correct. I consulted Dr Google and read that I should massage the bent legs several times a day and within a week the little billy kid was up and feeding beautifully from mother Willow.

We had fun thinking of names for the babies but none of us could agree until Jeremy suggested, 'Let's call them Harry and Meghan.' Everyone laughed and approved. Harry and Meghan it was. Willow proved to be an excellent first-time mother producing plenty of milk for her offspring. Their aunty Wisp was happy to share the goat shed with the two kids and all was well in the paddock.

After a couple of weeks Jeremy started to take off some of Willow's milk from her very full and lopsided udder to relieve the pressure from the distended side. He would tie Willow to the hay feeder and then crouch on the straw-covered floor and work at her udder, gently but firmly, until some of her milk squirted into the pan. This wasn't a very satisfactory arrangement and when I tried to milk Willow she wouldn't let her milk down for me. Who could blame her?

It was obvious that I didn't have the right technique. In desperation I telephoned a goat keeper in a nearby village and cheekily asked her if I might come and have some milking lessons. She generously agreed and let me sit at her side to learn.

'There are two methods and you need to find the right one for you,' she told me. 'It's difficult to explain but watch and then have a go.' She was patient with me and in control of her animals and, finally, after watching and trying a few times I managed to release a squirt of milk into the bucket and then another.

'Well done, now keep at it for a minute or two until there's no more milk left in the udder.' When I got home I felt more confident. My teacher had a purpose-built milking platform that her husband had designed and made for her. We definitely needed something like that for our goats. Jeremy and I looked on the internet and within a couple of weeks Jeremy had ordered the wood, designed our own milking platform and built it. The next task was to erect a small building to accommodate the milking platform and with enough room for a table, some feed bins and several bales of hay. Jeremy drew up the plans and when lockdown rules were eased, Chris came to The Gables and constructed it. Now we were all set to go with a milking parlour adjacent to the goat shed, a platform, a gleaming stainless steel bucket, a roll of udder wipes and some antiseptic cream for our hands. Daily milking could begin. The plan was to share the milk with the kids. We would take milk each morning and the rest of the time the kids could feed from their mother.

Some Golden Guernseys are born with horns and some are polled (born without). The father of the twins had horns and we wondered whether the kids would take after their father or their mother. Horns must be removed by a vet under anaesthetic but because of the National Lockdown we didn't have the option of the procedure. Both the kids were born with horns.

We definitely did not want to keep a billy goat at The Gables. Mature billy goats can be quite pungent during the mating season. The smell can taint the milk and besides which we didn't want Willow to be impregnated by her son which could result in birth defects. Harry was such a darling yet we needed to get rid of him without, we hoped, sending him to the great goat heaven in the sky. We placed an advert on an animal website offering Harry free to a good home. Jeremy didn't expect any responses so I was over the moon when a goat fanatic from Birmingham contacted us and was said she would be happy to rehome Harry. We arranged a date and Kelly, a tall and very friendly young woman in a hijab arrived with her husband and one of her children to collect little Harry and put him in the back of their four by four. Kelly told us in her broad Brummie accent, 'I'm goat mad and I've got 17 nanny and billy goats on an acre of scrubland just on the outskirts of Birmingham.'

Her husband gave me a weary look. 'She is completely obsessed with goats and she sends me to Morrisons three times a week to collect all the out-of-date fruit and veg.'

'How do you get it home?'

'I've got a pickup van and they let me take as much as I want so Kelly's goats eat everything from cabbages to melons. They must be the best-fed goats in the country.' We were delighted that little Harry was going to be in such kind and capable hands and a day after he left The Gables the lovely Kelly emailed us photos of Harry, who she had renamed Haroun, enjoying watermelon alongside his new friends. We were thrilled and relieved.

Now that Harry had gone and Meghan was growing up, Jeremy and I took it in turns to milk Willow, only doing so once a day in the morning. Jeremy listened to the Radio 4 news as he sat in the milking parlour whereas I played Willow country and gospel music. We would compare milk yields with Jeremy saying, 'You see Willow prefers to know what's going on in the world.'

'No, she's a country fan,' I countered if I got more milk than him. If I hadn't managed to get much milk that day I kept quiet. Sometimes I just sat on the milking platform and sang to Willow and looked out of the window at the changing seasons. It was a relaxing process and the nanny goat was patient and biddable as she stood munching food at one end whilst we milked her at the other.

Soon it was time to start using the milk. This involved buying more equipment – a stainless steel milk churn which we could store in the fridge, a stainless steel sieve which we lined with disposable liners every day to remove impurities such as stray pieces of hay and straw, and finally a milk thermometer which we would need if we were going to make cheese. Neither of us takes milk in our tea or coffee and we don't have cereal for breakfast so our milk consumption isn't very great. Willow was giving us over a litre of milk a day and we had to find a way to turn the milk into a product that we would eat. I tried soft cheese and cottage cheese but neither of us was particularly pleased with the results. Then I found a recipe for halloumi cheese which didn't require much expertise or equipment. Before too long I was making halloumi cheese at least twice a week, freezing what we didn't use and giving some away to friends. The cheese tasted particularly delicious once it had been chopped into cubes, fried in a dry pan and sprinkled with salt and lemon juice. Halloumi can be added to salads or roasted vegetables but I quite often ate the cheese straight from the stove because I found it so tempting.

When Meghan was weaned we decided to get Willow in kid again and hoped to do the same with Wisp. Goats come into season every three weeks during the autumn and winter and this is characterised by loud bleating, a red behind and a lot of agitation. As soon as the signs appear there is just a 12 hour window in which to mate and conceive. Willow came into season and we took her to the neighbouring village to meet a lovely Golden Guernsey billy goat stud who instantly took a shine to our girl. I felt a bit embarrassed to be holding Willow on a lead whilst her beau, Archie, nuzzled her ears and then mounted her but, fortunately, it was all over quickly and we took Willow back to The Gables where she began her next pregnancy. When Wisp showed the same signs we rushed her over to see Archie. Wisp, always much shyer than Willow, played hard to get. Eventually what had to take place did and we brought Wisp home. Unfortunately, three weeks later she came into season again. In consultation with Archie's owner we decided to bring him to stay for a few days during Wisp's next fertile spell. Sadly, she didn't 'take' and we gave up trying that year. Meanwhile Willow was getting bigger and bigger and at Shavuot 2021 when we had another group of friends staying with us to celebrate the festival, we all awoke to the birth of twin kids – a boy and a girl.

On the festival of Shavuot, in addition to the daily prayers we read the Book of Ruth. This is a story of a widow, Naomi, whose two sons die but whose childless daughters-in-law wish to remain at her side to comfort and care for her. She tries to persuade the young women to go back to their own people where they will have a chance to remarry and have children and one of them goes home whilst the other, Ruth, remains with her mother-in-law as they return to the ancestral home of Naomi. Naomi has a rich relative, Boaz, who falls in love with Ruth and they marry and from their lineage descends the famous King David.

This time all the children staying at The Gables were of one mind and there was a group decision. 'We've got to call them Ruth and Boaz,' our grandson announced. We agreed. In time Boaz became Bobo.

As before our Brummie goat lover agreed, when Bobo was weaned, to take him home to join her herd. We decided to keep Ruth who was the image of her mother Willow. We now had four nanny goats and we were milking once again.

Last summer we decided that we might be 'third time lucky' with Wisp and found another goat keeper a few miles away who had a pedigree stud billy goat. We made arrangements to take the three adult nanny goats, Willow, Wisp and Meghan, to meet the billy and stay at his smallholding for a few weeks so that all three girls could be served. Ruth was still too young to go so we would keep her at The Gables when the others went away. After we had made the arrangements the owner of the billy called to remind us that, 'You must produce a CAE certificate before I can let you onto my premises or if you prefer I can let my Billy goat come to stay at The Gables, but only if your girls are tested.' We had forgotten about this but it wasn't going to be difficult to arrange a test with our veterinary practice.

Caprine arthritis encephalitis (CAE) is a viral disease mainly affecting goats and occasionally sheep. Although the virus can remain dormant in the host animal, when the disease manifests itself the goat will develop painful, arthritic knee joints and mastitis leading to a distended and hardened udder. It is a nasty and debilitating condition. The British Goat Society recommends that all goat keepers test their goats at least once a year usually by a vet who takes a blood sample, then sends it to a laboratory where it is examined for antibodies. As with cows and the bovine tuberculosis (TB) test, any antibodies in the blood indicate that the animal is harbouring the virus even though it might never develop the disease. Unlike the test for bovine tuberculosis, goat testing is not mandatory but goat keepers take CAE seriously and we realised that without annual testing our girls would not be welcome in the goat world.

An appointment was made with our usual vets and one of them, a delightful and gentle Portuguese man, arrived on a late August afternoon accompanied by three students. We were entertaining in the courtyard when they pulled into the drive, baking pizzas in the wood-fired oven and enjoying the summer sunshine.

'Would you like to join us for some food?'

'When we've finished with the goats that would be lovely,' smiled Andre, the vet, and the students looked pleased at this unexpected invitation.

I took the group out to the goat shed and one by one the students extracted blood from the necks of the girls and marked each vial with the name of the goat. Job done, or so we assumed.

Back in the courtyard, before the vet and students arrived, I had been looking through a photo album that my friend Chrissie had brought with her. She had been a well-known dog breeder and Crufts judge in her younger days and when I mentioned this to the vet one of the students piped up,

'Dogs are my favourite animals.'

I quickly rearranged the seating so that Chrissie and the student could sit together and engage in 'doggie talk' whilst I rolled out pizza bases and loaded them and Jeremy cooked them in the oven. The pizzas cook in less than three minutes in the heat of the clay chamber and have a delicious, smoky taste. Eating outdoors always seems to increase appetites and as fast as I rolled and Jeremy baked there seemed to be an unending chorus of 'More please,' until finally the dough ran out and Jeremy and I were able to sit at the table and enjoy a well earned slice of halloumi topped pizza.

Three weeks later our vet called on my mobile.

'Gill, I'm so sorry but I have some bad news. Meghan has tested positive for CAE.'

It felt like déjà vu and, just as with the very healthy and glossy Beattie, Meghan looked in the pink and had shown absolutely no signs of the disease.

'Can we retest Andre? Is there a chance that it's a false positive?'

'You can if you want and we can send it to a different lab. There's one in Scotland that might give you a different result and quite quickly too. Shall we do that?'

A few days later all four goats were retested but this time not by students but quickly and efficiently by just one vet, who we hadn't met before.

'I really don't think that you'll get a different result but it's up to you. I'll chase it up as soon as possible and let you know.'

Sadly, when he called the following week the results confirmed the first diagnosis.

'What should I do? The goat society recommends immediate euthanasia. What do you think?'

'Well, if you keep her there are several disadvantages. The first is that she could spread the disease to the other three goats. The second is that you won't find a Golden Guernsey keeper who will either rent you a billy goat or let you onto their premises and the third thing I'd say is do it as quickly as possible because we need to wait another six months before we can test again. That allows for any disease to develop and to show up in the test.'

The die was cast and we knew that we didn't have a choice. Meghan would have to be destroyed even though she appeared perfectly healthy. We felt terribly sad for Meghan and her stablemates.

Not all slaughterhouses are the same. In Devon, 40 years ago, I can remember taking of one of our old sheep to the abattoir in the back of our Saab estate. As we got close to the facility the smell of the other animals coming from inside the building sent our girl into a spin. We both felt terrible and traitorous leaving the old sheep there to await what, we hoped, would be a swift end.

We had heard that there was a family-run abattoir here in Bedfordshire, less than half an hour's drive away, which had a good reputation. I called them and spoke to the owner's wife who ran the office. 'Goats and sheep have to be here by 7 am on Monday mornings. Will you be wanting the meat yourselves or will you be selling the goat to us?'

To my surprise we wouldn't have to pay for Meghan's destruction but would actually make a small return on her carcass, bless her.

The following Monday at 6 am by the light of a torch, we attached a lead to Meghan's collar and led her out of the goat shed and somehow or another managed to lift her onto the tail board of the Land Rover. I clambered in with Meghan and she rested her head in my lap for the whole journey. I stroked and talked to her, repeating again and again, 'You're such a lovely girl. Beautiful Meghan, you're a lovely, lovely girl.'

It was still deepest dark when we turned into the drive leading to a low-rise brick building adjacent to a field and some houses. Meghan jumped out of the Defender with me holding onto her lead whilst Jeremy went into the office to present the paperwork containing all the details of Meghan's unique animal ear tag number and our smallholding identification. When that was done we both walked Meghan into the building where, instead of fear, she showed great interest in the six Anglo Nubian goats standing in the pen in front of us. There was no smell of death and the people directing us were kind and polite and efficient. We left Meghan there, in her own pen, and drove home without talking as the sun began to rise.

A couple of days later my mobile rang and it was the lady from the abattoir who needed to clarify some details, 'Can you give me your bank details so that we can send you the proceeds of the sale of the meat.' Before we hung up I asked her,

'How long would Meghan have been waiting before she was dispatched?'

'Oh, no more than an hour.'

It was done, Meghan was no more and the other three goats took a week or two to revert to their usual inquisitive selves. Ruth, the youngest, who could often be found at the top of the wooden climbing frame in the paddock, didn't venture up there again for a while until her memories of Meghan had faded.

Now we had to wait six months before another CAE test could be conducted, but we didn't want to wait. The solution was to find a Golden Guernsey billy goat who was surplus to requirements and buy him in to service our small group of girls. We were making the assumption that none of ours was harbouring the virus and we would be saving an unwanted billy goat from an early demise.

'I'm not very keen on having a billy around the place,' I complained to Jeremy, 'They're big and smelly and they have nasty habits.'

'What's the alternative? If we wait another six months for the blood test and then five more months for them to kid and then three months to wean we will have lost another year before we can milk again and you won't be able to make any halloumi either.'

I accepted that we didn't really have a choice. We had to buy a billy or wait. We started looking.

Our local goat breeder put us in contact with another Golden Guernsey keeper who lives near Norwich and keeps a milking herd and some stud billies. She had rented out one of her young billies but his work was now done and he was destined for destruction. Hazel chatted with Jeremy by email and she happily agreed to sell us the billy goat rather than send him to the abattoir. We would have to drive over 60 miles to collect him as she was far too busy with her other goats to deliver him. Jeremy and Hazel agreed a price and fixed a date and we got ready for another bumpy journey to collect young Mr Billy from the village in Norfolk where he had been living for the past two months. The goat was in a shed across from a house which was in the process of being restored. The householder was very proud of the building. 'The walls are made of straw,' he told me. 'Did you know that straw is actually warmer and a better insulation than many modern materials and it isn't a fire risk?' It was an interesting project and I would have liked to have stayed longer to look around but our mission was to get the billy goat, attach a lead to his collar and get him into the Land Rover. 'He's very shy and we'll have a job to catch him,' said Hazel but in fact I put my hand out and managed to grab him and he came outside without any trouble. Jeremy and I heaved him up and put him in the back of the Defender where he immediately lay down on a cosy layer of straw whilst we all went inside to pay, fill in the paperwork and have the necessary cup of tea and comfort break before setting off on the return journey.

'You'll notice that he's got a funny horn and also a stub of a horn,' Hazel said with some embarrassment. I had noticed but didn't like to ask what had happened.

'I took the kid to the vet to have the horns removed but he botched the operation and to make matters worse the vet wouldn't refund my money even though I use him all the time.'

I thought that the horn looked quite attractive as if he was a fairytale Unicorn and I was pleasantly surprised with how pretty the billy looked. I had fallen for him already.

After completing the handover we headed home for The Gables. By the time we got back the three girls had sensed that something was in the air and they were waiting at the paddock gate to welcome the good looking young fellow. Within seconds the four of them were running around together and Wisp (the shy one) and Billy (unimaginatively named on the way home) had paired off and were making eyes at each other. Thoughts of Meghan seemed to have been forgotten.

From the moment that Billy arrived the girls didn't appear to come into season again and five months after his arrival the first kid was born to Willow, sired by a billy goat young enough to be her grandson!

It was the Sunday of the Coronation weekend and I had walked down to the village hall where a marquee had been erected on the field adjacent to the car park. Tea and cake was on offer and everyone was enjoying the excuse for a get-together. Jeremy had stayed at home keeping his eye on the livestock and digging trenches in which he was going to plant our main crop potatoes. The afternoon was as sunny as the Coronation Saturday had been wet and I was in my element, walking around and stopping to chat with village friends some of whom I hadn't seen for months. As I looked around I realised just how many people we knew and liked and how integrated we had become in the village. It was a lovely feeling and I felt truly blessed. Just as I was talking to Ken and Thelma my phone pinged with a message from Jeremy who had been out in the goat shed checking on Willow who looked as though she had begun her labour that morning. He had found her sitting with a new born kid. 'Ping' he sent a photo and wrote, 'It's a billy and he's perfect.'

I walked around proudly showing the photograph to anyone who was interested.

'He's beautiful,' said Judy, 'Well done Willow.'

'I'll see him when I come in on Wednesday,' Dianne said as I ran over to show her the picture.

'I'm going home to see the baby.' I made a quick round of the tables and set off at a smart pace. As soon as I got through the door I ran upstairs, took off my glad rags and put on my old working clothes and wellies and rushed out to congratulate the mother and admire the new arrival.

It was a perfect ending to a sunny Bank Holiday Sunday and we didn't have long to wait for the next surprise.

The following day we got up and began our morning round, opening up the chicken houses, scattering corn, filling up all the animal buckets with fresh water and, finally, going to the goat shed to check on

Willow and her baby. To our surprise and delight Ruth was sitting by the open door surrounded by two white kids. Ruth and the twins stood up as we approached and the kids began feeding from their mother. We were thrilled with the three little goats and especially pleased that neither Willow nor Ruth had required our help with their deliveries.

'What shall we call them?'

'Let me think about it for a day or two.' Jeremy always likes to consider matters rather than making a snap decision.

I had a flash of inspiration.

'No need to think. The boy is called Charlie and the twins are Diana and Camilla.'

'You can't be serious,' Jeremy rolled his eyes as we stood looking at the kids, 'I'm not calling them after that lot.'

My mind was made up and I closed the goat house door so that we and the goats were all inside together.

'I am not opening this door until you agree to my idea. They're brilliant names and everyone but you will love them.'

Jeremy looked at me and burst out laughing.

'OK I know when I'm beaten. Charlie, Diana and Camilla it is. Now open up and let's go back to the house and have a cup of tea.'

Two goats had safely delivered and now there was just one to go. Wisp, who had never managed to get pregnant before, definitely looked in the family way with a large belly and a swollen udder.

A whole week later Wisp began her labour. It was difficult and long and I spent several hours with her in the goat shed stroking and encouraging her to push. Jeremy joined us every half an hour and finally, with Wisp exhausted and sitting on the straw, the head and feet began to emerge. She was so tired that Jeremy helped by gently pulling the baby as the nanny pushed with her last remaining strength. Wisp remained sitting and the baby made weak noises and we used a towel to dry her off as her mother was too weak to lick her clean. After a while, with the other goats and kids running in and out of the shed, we decided to move mother and newborn to the milking parlour for a quiet night away from the clumsy kids. It wasn't looking good for Wisp or her baby and I was worried (as usual) and Jeremy was stoic and said, 'Let's wait and see how they are in the morning.'

Early the next day we opened the milking parlour with trepidation. Mother and baby were lying together on the straw and we managed to get Wisp to stand. I looked at Jeremy and said, 'If you hold Wisp I'll try to put baby on her teat.'

Some months earlier we had called the vet to see and treat Wisp, who had developed an abscess on one side of her udder. 'I'm not sure that she will be able to feed any kids,' the vet had said. 'You'll have to wash out the udder every day with this solution and give her some injections. It might be okay at the end of her treatment but there's no guarantee that the udder will ever produce milk.'

It didn't and now we had a problem. Kids and lambs and calves, just like human babies, need colostrum in the first 24 hours of life. This is the thick and enriched milk that the mothers produce to feed their newborns. We keep a box of colostrum sachets for rejected or poorly lambs and we decided to give the kid some lamb colostrum to get her started with the hope that Wisp would regain her strength and take over the feeding. The kid was hungry and took to the bottle immediately. Wisp couldn't feed her although she was fiercely protective of her precious little coffee-coloured offspring. Mother and daughter were identical in colour whereas Ruth and Willow (both white Golden Guernseys) had produced kids with white coats like themselves.

'I'm going to milk Willow,' pronounced Jeremy. 'She's always been a good milker and as she's only feeding one kid she might have some spare milk for baby.'

Good old Willow allowed herself to be led into the milking parlour and she let down a litre of precious milk which we proceeded to feed the kid over the course of the next 24 hours. I ordered a large bag of powdered goat replacement milk, washed, rinsed and sterilised the lamb bottles and we were back bottle-feeding just as we had been a few months earlier with the poddy – rejected – lambs. Although it sometimes feels like a chore for the most part it is one of my great pleasures. Several times a day I warm a bottle and have the opportunity to cuddle a lamb, stroke it and usually give it a few kisses. They grow up fast and within a few weeks the lamb is feeding from a bucket and doesn't want any more of my mothering. This little kid, who we called Baby, stood in between my legs as I sat on a bale of straw and placed the bottle in her mouth which she sucked eagerly. It didn't take long and gave me the chance to pet the little one without having to chase her round the paddock.

Another problem arose the next day after we put Wisp and the kid back with the rest of the herd. Baby began to limp and was lifting her right front leg off the ground.

'Jeremy come and see this. I think one of the other kids must have been playing with Baby and hurt her by accident by jumping on top of her. Shall I call the vet?'

'Don't be ridiculous she'll be better tomorrow.'

She wasn't better and was unable to put any weight on her hoof at all. I decided to take matters into my own hands and called the vet who arrived that afternoon and examined her.

'I don't think she has broken it or been damaged by the others. The knee joint is hot and swollen. This little kid has septic arthritis of the knee.'

'How did she get it?'

'Feel her navel. It's also swollen. She probably got it from dirty straw that she was lying on when she was born. The infection went into her blood through the navel and has given her a septic knee joint. If this happens another time when a goat is struggling to give birth you need to sterilize the umbilicus and that prevents infections getting in.'

'Will she be alright?'

Ever the pessimist and worrier I was very upset to hear the vet pronounce his diagnosis. I also felt guilty because in helping Wisp to give birth we might have mishandled the situation and actually caused the infection.

'I'm going to give her an antibiotic shot and an anti-inflammatory injection and then you'll have to give her the injections yourselves for another seven days. Keep the kid and her mother away from the others in a separate barn and if she doesn't respond we could do some surgery. But there's no guarantee that the surgical procedure will work and if it doesn't she won't have any quality of life.'

We sighed, we took the syringes, we looked at each other and I knew that Jeremy thought she would recover whereas I was sure she was a goner.

We dutifully carried out the injections together and for the first day or two we barely saw any change in Baby's condition. Then, on the third day she began to put some weight on her bad leg and by the time we had finished all her shots Baby seemed fully recovered. We moved Wisp and the kid back to the goat shed and Baby was soon running around the paddock with the other three kids, climbing the children's slide, staying close to her mother when she wanted reassurance and protection from the others and bounding over to me to feed from the bottle several times a day. In my eyes it was a miracle. In Jeremy's opinion it was simply what he, ever the optimist, had predicted would happen. I was delighted to be proved wrong.

Now there was the problem of Billy, the father of the kids. When we bought Billy he had been destined for the knacker's yard. Our purchase gave him eight more months of a blissful existence with Ruth and Willow and Wisp in a lush, green paddock with a nightly bucket of tasty concentrates. Now Billy was surplus to requirements and had started to become a bit of a menace. He regularly broke into the chicken run where he jumped onto the hen house roof and damaged it. We didn't want the nanny goats getting pregnant again for at least the next eighteen months, so we advertised Billy on the animal website. There were no takers. I telephoned the goat lover in Birmingham.

'Hello Kelly, do you remember me?'

'Of course! We still have Bobo and about 15 other goats.'

'What's that noise I can hear in the background?'

'Oh, yes its's a bit busy here. I'm opening a shop at the back of our house and I'm going to sell chicken and meat as well as other things. And I'm learning to butcher.'

'Can a woman slaughter animals under Islamic law?' I was genuinely surprised as I wasn't sure if it would be allowed in Jewish law and had never heard of a female ritual slaughterer.

'Yes we can as long as we say the prayer before the killing.'

'I'm impressed. Well, you might want our Billy goat for your shop. If not we will take him here to the local abattoir. Have a chat with your husband and let me know tomorrow.'

'I will. By the way are you able to supply me with chickens? I'm having terrible trouble finding free-range, organic chickens.'

'I'm not surprised. Since all the trouble with avian flu and then with the rise in energy costs and feed lots of people have decided to give up keeping chickens.'

'Could you supply me with 20 or 30 a week?'

I laughed.

'We keep a few chickens but we aren't breeding them commercially or for sale. Sorry Kelly.'

'No worries, just thought I'd ask. Keep me in mind when you're next selling goats or giving them away. Lovely to hear from you.'

'Lovely to speak with you too and good luck with the shop and the butchering.'

The next day Kelly and I exchanged messages. Her husband had decided that they were too busy trying to get the shop ready and couldn't drive down to Bedfordshire to collect one goat. It was the right call.

We had no choice. I telephoned the local family-run abattoir, twenty minutes ride away, the same one we had taken Meghan to some six months earlier.

'Yes, bring him in. Any Monday morning before 7 am. Do you want the meat back or are we buying the meat from you?'

'Buying it like you did last time please.'

At 5 am on a bright June morning, I rose with a heavy heart. I fed the other animals as Jeremy backed the Land Rover into the field where Billy was waiting in the sheep barn, where he had slept for the previous two nights. He had no idea why he had been separated from his women but he was calm and biddable as we led him out and up into the Defender. I jumped into the back where I sat with Billy as he settled down by my side for his final journey.

'Ready? Are you alright there in the back?'

'Yes, let's get going.'

I stroked Billy all the way to the abattoir and he never once attempted to stand or pull away from me. When we arrived he jumped down eagerly and we led him into the facility where he was put in a pen behind six sheep.

'Take off his lead and collar and then come into the office, please, to fill in the paperwork.'

There was no noise, no smell of death and all was calm in the early morning light of a beautiful summer's day. Billy would soon be in goat heaven leaving behind his four offspring and their mothers. We drove back in an empty car knowing that by the time we arrived home for our cup of tea and coffee the deed would be done. Thank you Billy, your work was complete and you have left behind four fabulous kids.

CHAPTER TWELVE -
SUCCOT THE FEAST OF
TABERNACLES AND THE BIRDS

Five days after the solemnity and rigour and intense spirituality of Yom Kippur we celebrate another festival, Succot – the Feast of Tabernacles – which lasts eight days

This is one of the three pilgrimage festivals which includes Pesach – Passover, and Shavuot – Pentecost. In Temple times Jews who could were obliged to travel to Jerusalem to deliver animals to the priests who officiated in the Temple and oversaw and performed the ritual sacrifices

Since the destruction of both Temples, the last in 70 CE, there is no longer a religious obligation to appear in Jerusalem. Yet many Israeli Jews and those from around the world still choose to visit Jerusalem for the pilgrimage festivals, gathering to stand and pray by the small remaining portion of the ancient Temple, the Western (or Wailing) Wall. Perhaps, as they gaze up at the stones, they are remembering their history or hoping for the building of the third and final Temple.

As in an orthodox synagogue there is a division at the Wall too with men on one side of the fence and women on the other. I have stood beside those ancient stones many a time and been moved to tears watching the women in fervent prayer. Some are begging to be blessed with children, others are praying for the recovery from illness for themselves or a relative. Women cry openly or rest a forehead on their arm as they lean into the Wall hoping that it will absorb their pain and bring them solace. Joy and sorrow stand side by side in this historic place. I could stay there for hours, sitting on one of the white plastic chairs placed in the shade for those who wish to take the weight off their feet, just observing and thinking and, of course sometimes, praying. It is a cornucopia of sounds and sights and colours and cultures. Requests written on tiny scrolls of paper are pressed into the cracks between the stones and high above them nesting pigeons and doves look down on all and coo oblivious to the murmurings below. Female soldiers of the Israel Defense Forces in army fatigues with guns strapped to their backs stand next to orthodox women who, even in the heat of summer, are dressed modestly in tops that cover their arms to the wrists and skirts below the knee, wearing thick tights and, if married, wigs or snoods. Orthodox married women are not supposed to show their hair – their crowning glory – to anyone except their husband and children and in spite of the discomfort in the heat of the Middle East they adhere to these strictures.

It is not only Jews who flock to this ancient site but Christians of all denominations, some from Africa in brightly-coloured dresses and headscarves, born-again Americans often with their loudly spoken guides, and visitors from all around the world. Japanese groups walk underneath open umbrellas to protect them from the sun and there are hippies and beggars and lost souls, some who have been touched by the Jerusalem Syndrome.

This condition, well-recognised and studied since the 1930s and even mentioned in the Middle Ages, is known to exist in a number of forms. Sufferers begin to dress in biblical clothing and identify with figures from the Old or New Testament, sometimes walking the streets preaching or singing religious hymns. During the years 1980 to 1993, 1,200 tourists were assessed at the Kfar Shaul Mental Health Centre in Jerusalem with severe Jerusalem-themed mental health problems. Of the 100 tourists seen at the Centre each year the majority are Christians, some are Jews, and a smaller number are Muslims. Although a significant proportion of these people already had an underlying mental health disorder, others developed the psychosis after they arrived in the city. Once treated with sedatives and counselling and removed from Jerusalem and its holy places the condition usually abated.

On the men's side of the Wall there is an even more marked contrast between those standing and davening – praying – or those who are just looking on and taking in the scene and the historic site. There will be Israelis with knitted kippot – small crocheted caps – denoting that they are dati leumi adherents of the national religious persuasion and orthodox in their observance. Soldiers dressed in different-coloured boots and berets which identify their regiments, stand in groups with their units praying and perhaps remembering that in 1967 this area was captured by their predecessors during the Six Day War. Men in black velvet kippot are usually dressed in trousers and shirts distinct from the more casual t-shirts and chinos of their dati leumi counterparts. Their prayers will be the same but perhaps their politics and lifestyle will be less similar. Then there are the men dressed in the garb of 18th century Polish aristocracy, the adherents of the Chassidic movement that swept through large parts of Eastern Europe and caused a split in the orthodox world at that time. These men follow one particular Rebbe or rabbinic leader and they will be known as Chassidim of that Rebbe's movement. The Rebbe, as distinct from a pulpit rabbi who ministers to a single congregation in one specific synagogue, is a leader of a movement which includes thousands of families and their descendants. The Rebbe will have received the mantle of leadership from his father or grandfather and usually this passes to his heir with the Rebbe seen as a bridge between the Almighty and his followers. Some Rebbes have many adherents around the world but most live in America or Israel, Canada and the UK even though the Rebbe might live in a different country from his flock. The Chassidim look to their spiritual leader for guidance in matters of religion and behaviour and will often ask for direction in earthly matters such as starting a business or advice with personal problems. The Rebbe's bracha – blessing – will be sought for many reasons such as recovery from illness, for success in finding a marriage partner or being granted children.

The dress of Chassidic men will, to the untrained eye, not differ greatly and all wear black coats, black hats trimmed with fur for the high holy and festival days and the Sabbath, and plain black hats for the rest of the week. On the Sabbath and Holy Days the followers of the Gerer Rebbe wear brimless fur hat known as a spodik. Recently, because of the high cost of real fur spodiks, which can cost several thousand pounds, the Grand Rebbe of Ger has declared that his followers are only allowed to buy spodiks made of fake fur. Married men who are followers of the Belzer Rebbe wear high white knee socks for the festivals but long black knee socks for the Sabbath. The Chassidic sects of Chabad and Karlin never wear high socks. The followers of the Skver Rebbe wear long leather boots for the High Days and Holy Days. On the Sabbath, festivals and at weddings married men will wear a type of frock coat, called a bekishe, which is made of black silk or polyester. All the men have payot, ringleted side curls in front of their ears following the biblical injunction that a man should not cut the corners of his beard. A few wear their striped prayer shawls over their black coats and, as with the women, they make no concession to the burning heat but follow the tradition that the leader of their movements set back in der heim – the old country. Most of these men, even if they are Israeli citizens, will refuse to serve in the army and many spend their days in 'learning' poring over the Talmud and its commentaries and loudly and devotedly debating the answers in pairs for hours on end. They pray intently but when they walk they move quickly as if wasting any second away from study is a misuse of their time on earth. Although some have gainful employment as teachers, many of these men are supported by their wives who go out to work and also manage to care for often very large families. All humankind is here at the Wall and I am fascinated by the place and never more so than at festival times, particularly Succot when every balcony and courtyard is filled with the temporary booths and shelters in which Jews are supposed to eat all their meals and even sleep during the week of festivities.

Here in Bedfordshire the festival coincides with the beginning of autumn and often the weather is wet and windy. Nonetheless we are obliged to erect a Succah – a temporary shelter – topped with leaves and rush matting. The Succah reminds us of the 40 years of wandering in the desert when the Israelites followed Moses from their liberation from slavery in Egypt until they entered the Promised Land. The nomads in the wilderness never lived in permanent houses so we too take our meals outside in our flimsy tabernacles and wooden structures for all the days of Succot. We do not, however, attempt to sleep in our Succah. It's just too cold.

'Mum, Dad,' our kids used to moan when they were teenagers and we were living in London, 'Why are there so many festivals crammed into such a short period of time. How are we supposed to pass our exams when we keep being off school and in the synagogue?'

'We all managed to get our A levels and even degrees whilst keeping the festivals and Shabbat, so you can do it too,' we would reply. I'm happy to report that they managed to finish their education and also had fun inviting friends into our Succah and visiting theirs where all the parents ensured that there was a good supply of nosh and soft drinks to keep the teenagers happy.

It's true that this month of feasting and fasting and building and entertaining can be quite taxing especially when children are trying to catch up with schoolwork and adults need to earn a living. Somehow or another we manage to get through this month of festivities. Once we are outside sitting in our Succah with friends and family, laughing at the craziness of eating meals whilst wearing coats and hats to keep us warm and buoyed by the drinking of wine and whisky it is fun and wonderful and joyful.

We put up our Succah in the courtyard next to the barn. It is really a small marquee whose roof is replaced by wooden slats which are covered with boughs of laurel and through which we can see the stars. This structure can accommodate 30 or more at a pinch and at the beginning of the festival we have had it full with friends and family who come and stay at The Gables. The two days at the beginning of the eight days of the festival are Holy Days when we pray and feast and do not go to work. The last two days of the festival are also holy. In between we have several evenings when we can entertain local friends and invite them to come and sit in our Succah. The first time I had to explain what on earth we were doing and why but by the end of the evening everyone agreed with my nearest neighbour, Sharon, when she said, 'Thank you. I thought it was a mad idea but it's been great fun and I hope you'll invite us next year.'

The very next year the rain came down in torrents and Faye, another neighbour and friend, looked at me in horror, 'Surely we can't sit outside in this?'

'Don't worry. The rule is that if the quantity of water dripping through and off the roof is going to make porridge soggy then we can go indoors.'

After a few minutes, wet and laughing, eight of us trooped inside and spent the evening eating and drinking, talking and making merry in the warmth of the barn.

Not only does the festival remind us of ancient times when our ancestors lived in precarious conditions, wandering from place to place until they were able to settle permanently but it also has a vital lesson to teach us today. We see on our television screens the millions of people displaced by wars and famines and earthquakes. All of these poor souls survive in tents and cobbled-together structures often for years. They might never be blessed to reach their Promised Land but we, here in Bedfordshire, experience this for only eight days and we do not even have to sleep outdoors. We have an alternative to the Succah – a weather-proof house. Amongst the bonhomie and rejoicing we try to remember those refugees and their plight and acknowledge that we too can, in just a moment, have our lives turned upside down as we did during the Covid pandemic. None of us is immune from upheaval and tragedy however much we fortify our houses and we Jews should know this only too well having been forced out so many times from places that we called home.

Five years ago we were sitting in the Succah on the first night of the festival. Every few moments an eerie shrieking sound would emanate from the ash tree overlooking the garage. I went outside and there, on a branch, was a barn owl calling with its piercing cry. The bird continued to screech throughout the evening. It hasn't happened again but it is a memory that remains each year when I take my seat in the Succah under the stars.

Birds have been and continue to be a delight and wonder at The Gables and in the surrounding countryside. When we left London we had watched, at first with pleasure and later with horror, as our garden bird feeder attracted feral parakeets who proceeded to frighten all the smaller birds away. They were and are a plague that has not yet arrived in Bedfordshire but, sadly, I saw a solitary parakeet flying over our field two years ago. I wondered about getting a shotgun licence and some shooting lessons!

The numerous buzzards and red kites and kestrels thrill me as much today as they did when first we moved to the countryside. In the 1980s the red kite was a threatened species in the UK. They had been hunted almost to extinction over a 200 year period. Between 1990 and 1994 a small number of red kites were introduced in the Chiltern Hills, a few pairs were from Wales but most came from the Navarra region of Spain with the last ten pairs in 1994 from the Spanish area of Aragon. Today there are at least 2000 breeding pairs throughout the country and this has been one of the most successful reintroduction programmes in the world. In fact, ten years on from our relocation to The Gables, I see far more red kites overhead than I do buzzards. The plucky crows mob the red kites and buzzards, chasing them away from their territories even though they are so much smaller than the birds of prey they are pursuing. I never understand why this works but the larger creatures turn tail and flee from the corvids.

Kestrels, too, are abundant and they can be spotted hovering over fields or roads, their eyesight trained on potential prey below. Wings flapping, while keeping their bodies still as their head and neck point downwards, they are able to stay in the air for half a minute or more. Recently a female kestrel was a regular visitor in our field. She would perch on top of the fence post next to gate and then swoop down to pick up food from the field. The bird has disappeared for now and I hope that she is nesting nearby and will have a successful brood. Kate, across the road, had a kestrel in a nest box high up on one of her trees five years ago. The mother hatched several chicks and Kate called me to, 'Come over with your camera and take a few photos.'

'They're fabulous aren't they?' I gushed having never seen a nesting kestrel or her young before. The following year some crows invaded the nest and smashed the eggs before they could hatch. The kestrels did not return the next year, nor can they now as the box was detached from the tree during a storm and has not been replaced. There is a war going on in the trees and skies for space and food and territorial rights and the winner takes all.

Under our pergola we have a nesting box used by blue tits every spring but, try as I might, I have never seen them fledge. There is also a Victorian letterbox fixed to a wall at the back of the house, a relic from from the previous owner. It too is a favourite site for nesting tits but I do wonder how the baby birds manage to jump up and post themselves out into the world when they are ready to fly. Mother Nature holds back her secrets and keeps me guessing. There is always danger in our garden and I can't deny that Nigel and even little Mabel catch a number of small birds and often pigeons. Beware the pigeon that stops too close to the house on the raised beds filled with brassicas. Nigel waits and pounces and we find white and grey feathers strewn near the site of the murder which we have to clear up before some of our more squeamish visitors spot them.

These are just some of our regular birds but from time to time grey-legged geese alight in the pasture looking for suitable nesting sites. Numerous brightly-plumed pheasant cocks wander around the perimeter of the field followed by a dull-coloured harem of hens. Pheasants, which are native to Asia, were introduced into much of Europe by the Romans arriving in Britain with the Normans in the 11th century. Unlike many of our British birds they do not mate for life nor manage even one season of fidelity. The larger and more brilliantly-coloured the male pheasant is the more likely there is to be a harem of brown-feathered females trailing behind him. The ladies might flock to the male but the cock pheasant is not a streetwise bird and many a carcass attests to his inability to navigate country roads. He is as stupid as he is vain but I am a sucker for his beautiful colouring and slow, imperial walk. Pheasants were nearly extinct until, in the 19th century, they became a popular game bird and they are extensively reared by gamekeepers. According to the League Against Cruel Sports up to 146,000 pheasants are shot in the UK every day during the hunting season. I am glad to provide a refuge for those who escape and 'go native'.

Occasionally a green woodpecker will land in the paddock and dig for ants in the long grass and fat red-legged partridges wander just too far away for a good camera shot. Four years ago, on a foggy autumn morning, I thrilled to the sight of two cattle egrets who stopped in the field probably thrown off course by fog. I was able to photograph and film them.

When I first went into Kate's kitchen we sat at her wooden table and drank a cup of coffee whilst her elderly Alsatian rescue dog, Sky, sat at our feet. As we chatted about her animals and garden I looked up and noticed several bird feeders positioned just in front of the kitchen window. 'They're very close to the house. Will the birds really come and feed from them?'

'Yes, if you don't disturb them they'll fly to and from the food and I have my own private bird show.' I went home and told Jeremy and we copied the idea. As I wash the dishes at the kitchen sink I look out of the window and watch goldfinches, long tailed tits, robins, great tits and blue tits alight on the feeders. The little birds are constantly turning this way and that on the lookout for predators as they nibble the seeds and peck at the logs of suet that we hang from a hollowed out piece of wood. A second feeder beside the driveway near the gate attracts greater spotted woodpeckers and chaffinches and another seed holder in the back garden is a magnet for sparrows, dunnocks and robins. Out of sight, but very vocal by day are song thrushes and little owls whose distinctive squeak we hear less often. At night tawny owls call with their trade mark twit twoo. Pied wagtails appear in the summer and nest in the sheep barn, carving small hollows in the hay where they lay their eggs. Swifts and swallows arrive in late spring and early summer. I am envious of Kate who is visited by swallows who come back to nest in her stables year after year. On my daily walk I spot skylarks rising from the fields, ascending vertically until they are just a dot in the sky although their song can still be heard after they disappear from sight.

Coming from London where I was used to seeing pigeons, blackbirds, starlings and parakeets, I am delighted to find such a wide variety of birdlife at The Gables and to glimpse the rare visitor, such as a bullfinch which I have only seen twice in ten years. One day when our Wednesday walking group was passing by a hedge on Honeydon Road, Ken called out, 'Look there's a yellowhammer,' as a flash of bright yellow flashed past us. 'There used to be so many of them when I was a child,' he said sadly.

Heather pointed out, 'Lapwings over there in the field,' on another of our other Wednesday walks. They have a distinctive high pitched call and equally exotic tall head plumage.

In the winter, fieldfares and red wings arrive from Scandinavia and hundreds of them alight on our field day after day, sometimes roosting in the walnut trees turning the bare branches into living sculptures. They are most welcome.

When I visit London I am amazed to find that crows and blackbirds will stand almost next to me on paths as I walk by. They show no fear of humans. Nor do urban foxes who strut around in broad daylight without a care in the world. Friends and family have to make sure to close patio windows in London or risk finding a fox sitting in their kitchens or on their lounge sofas. Foxes are more wary of country folk and with good reason – farmers have shotguns.

These are just some of the wild delights of country living but there are also the joys (and sometimes challenges) of keeping domestic poultry.

Back in Devon 40 years ago, we raised hens and ducks and enjoyed their eggs. Here at The Gables we started our poultry collection with some fat, french faverolle hens that we purchased from a breeder down the A1 in Biggleswade. We added an impressive rooster to the run and named him Joe Cockerel. The hens produced delicious brown eggs and we soon had enough for all our weekly cooking and baking. Gradually we added more birds. Some of them were cast-offs from families who realised that they could no longer keep poultry in their urban back gardens. Six beautiful, white silkie birds came from a woman in Norfolk who had kept them as pets. She wasn't able to look after them when she returned to full-time work but she was anxious to send them to a good home. Along with the birds came a list of foods that they liked and a handwritten letter in which she asked us to, 'Please feed my babies sweetcorn, cheese and freshly cooked greens. The biggest of the girls is called Fairy and she is my special favourite.' I tore up the list. These prima donnas would have to muck in with our girls and eat corn and layers mash like the rest of the flock. They not only survived this change in regime but thrived and nested and produced silky-textured pale cream eggs and also plenty of baby silkie chicks. Then we were gifted two bantams – a small sized hen with feathery feet – by a family in Bedford that had been hand-fed by the children.

'Please will you take the birds?' asked the father. 'We didn't realise that our neighbours would object to the noise and we can't bear the thought of killing the hens.' We took them in but the children were nearly in tears when they left. 'You have visiting rights. Come and see them whenever you want,' Jeremy told them. A year after we took the bantams these children used an incubator to raise some quails from tiny eggs that they bought in Bedford market. 'Could you,' asked the dad apologetically when he called us, 'Possibly take the quails as we haven't anywhere to keep them? We thought we would be moving to a bigger house but the sale fell through.'

Quails are not like chickens. They are mentioned in the Old Testament in the Book of Numbers when the Israelites complain to the Lord that they are fed up with eating the Manna which arrives on the ground for them each morning. They moan that they want meat and God tells them that they will have so much quail meat to eat that it will come out of their nostrils and it does. Yuck! Quails never appealed to me after that and they proved to be quite a problem when we agreed to take them from the Bedford family. It isn't possible to free-range quails because once they are outdoors they either run or fly away and never return so we put them in a barn and lined the sides with netting to keep the birds from escaping. We didn't know which were male or even if there were any females until one day we found three small pebbles in the barn. They were quail eggs which are, apparently, a delicacy and command a high price in the shops. Give me a hen egg any day. To my mind a tiny quail offering is hardly worth the trouble of boiling and peeling! We hoped that the quails would go broody but they did not. Instead we put 20 of their tiny eggs under a nesting hen and 18 days later the eggs began to hatch and we were congratulating ourselves on a successful experiment in bird surrogacy. However, within an hour or two the quail chicks began to die. I Googled furiously and discovered that hens and quails do not speak the same language. It was down to me to rescue the last six babies and teach them how to eat and drink. Our grandson's bedroom was the obvious place to raise the birds as it was the smallest room in the house and could be heated to the high temperature that the chicks required. Six jam jar lids were filled with chick crumbs and water and every hour I place the tiny beaks of the tiny birds into the food and water and willed them to learn how to eat and drink. It was unbearably hot in the nursery and when our granddaughter visited a couple of weeks later she declared, 'Grandma it stinks in here.' My friend Heather came to see the dots as she called them as they weren't much bigger than a large tiddly wink. Remarkably five of the six birds survived, grew and eventually joined the rest of the flock in the quail barn. When the birds began to die from old age we all agreed that we would not be raising quails again.

Geese are entirely different. Jeremy purchased a crateful of white Embden geese from a local breeder two years after we arrived in Bedfordshire. The geese went to live on the pond at the far end of the vegetable garden and Chris and Jeremy put up a goose shed on a small 'island' accessed by a wooden drawbridge. The geese are as elegant as swans when swimming. They may look beautiful but they are aggressive creatures with sharp serrated beaks and tongues. Some people even use them as guard dogs because they hiss at strangers and will bite them if they get within range. I learnt to enter the goose enclosure with a stick in my hand in case one of the birds took me to be an intruder.

Once bitten twice shy and I had the marks on my thigh to prove it and I took no more chances. In the spring the female geese began to lay the most enormous white eggs in the straw inside the shed. Eventually one of the birds decided to sit on the eggs and we started counting off the 35 day incubation period. The bigger the bird the longer it takes to hatch. Quails only take 18 days, ducks 21 days, hens 28 days and our big Embdens should have hatched after 35 days but our sitting goose got bored and got up after a couple of weeks and went into the pond to swim with the rest of the flock. The opportunistic crows then moved in and stole all the eggs and we continued to fight a daily war to collect any newly-laid eggs before the thieves flew off with them.

I complained to Heather and wondered if she had any ideas. 'What can I do about my geese? They just won't sit for long enough. They lose patience and get up and I don't think we will ever breed goslings at The Gables,'

'My dad was a proper countryman and he used to put goose eggs under broody hens.' Heather smiled as she remembered her father and her childhood

'Really. But goose eggs are enormous how was that possible?'

'Well, he did and usually under little bantams. You'll find that bantams are the best sitters.'

I went home and told Jeremy and we both decided that the next year we would give it a try. We had the two Bedford bantams from the children in town and they had been excellent sitters and mothers of chicks and the following spring we put four goose eggs under the two birds. 35 days later three out of the four hatched into fluffy, yellow goslings. The mothers were so proud to have produced such fine, big chicks and the goslings believed that the hens were their mothers and followed them around the chicken run and hid under the wings of the birds until the goslings just became too big to hide any more. When the goslings turned from yellow to white with their adult feathers and large orange webbed feet, we slowly introduced them to the flock at the pond where they joined their biological tribe.

I was excited to see Heather the next day at our Wednesday morning walk. 'Heather, it really works. Although hens and quails don't understand each other it seems that hens and geese do. We will try that again. It's amazing.'

Heather smiled at me and chuckled. 'I'm delighted. Yes, Dad had lots of old fashioned country knowledge. I wonder whether our children or grandchildren will know about all these old ways?' She sighed, a rueful expression crossing her face.

'I don't suppose they will but your dad knew what he was doing and I've learnt a useful lesson. Jeremy and I are really grateful. Would you like a gosling?' She sensibly shook her head. 'Absolutely not!' And with that our group set off on our weekly walk, chatting away and putting the world to rights as we always did.

The following year we tried the trick again and each successive year we have put goose eggs under hens and been rewarded. There is a limit to the size of flock that we want and we sell any surplus geese and exchange their eggs for poultry food at the local farm shop where customers are prepared to pay £2 for one goose egg. I decided that we should try to cook one of our own goose eggs but when I opened it I found there was a huge blood spot inside and I felt sick. Jews are not allowed to eat an egg which contains a blood spot because this indicates that a new embryo is forming and it is forbidden to eat an embryo.

Jews are also forbidden from eating birds of prey or birds that scavenge. Game birds are not allowed because they are usually killed by shooting but if they were killed in a kosher manner by a shochet – a man who is trained in the ritual killing of animals in the kosher manner – they would be permitted. Jews have a mesora – a tradition – for eating certain birds which include chickens, partridges, ducks, quails, pheasants, geese, pigeons and doves. In more recent times turkeys have been sanctioned as kosher birds and added to the list.

We are not allowed to eat the eggs from a bird that is not kosher such as a crow or a heron nor can we drink the milk from non-kosher animals such as pigs or camels. Meat from kosher animals, killed according to kosher ritual practices must also have the blood removed before cooking. This koshering process involves soaking the flesh in clean water for 30 minutes and then draining it. Thereafter the meat is salted and left for 60 minutes. It is then washed three times in cold water to remove the salt and then the meat is kosher.

I can remember watching my mother kasher meat and chicken when I was a child. On the small balcony of our flat she kept a bucket in which she soaked the meat and later rinsed off the salt. Nowadays the kashering is carried out by kosher butchers in their shops or in kosher meat factories and I doubt that many of my generation and anyone younger would know how to carry out the procedure.

The prohibition against eating blood is so engrained from childhood that I have never wanted to contravene this law. Given these rules it is even more strange that the infamous blood libels of the Middle Ages were believed. The blood libel is a horrific myth whose origins began in Norwich in 1144 when the Jews of the city were falsely accused, without any evidence, of the ritual slaughter and crucifixion of a boy, William, who was found at Easter time murdered in the woods. All the Norwich Jews were taken into protection by the local sheriff, John de Chesney, who advised the community that the ecclesiastical courts had no jurisdiction over them. The Jews were answerable only to King Stephen who dismissed the baseless charges and when the situation had calmed down the Jews went back to their homes. A Benedictine monk, Thomas of Monmouth, arrived in Norwich five years after the unsolved murder and wrote a book claiming that there was an annual meeting of Jews to decide which local community would kill a Christian child. His evidence was based on the words of a Jew who had converted to Christianity and wanted to ingratiate himself with his new brethren. Subsequently several unsolved child murders were blamed on Jews in Gloucester (1168), Bury St Edmunds (1181) and Bristol (1183) and the most infamous of them all the death of Little St Hugh of Lincoln who went missing in 1255 and for which 19 Jews were executed by the order of King Henry III. The blood libel spread to continental Europe and beyond, adding that Jews kill Christian children to drain their blood and mix it with flour to make matzos – the unleavened bread – which they eat at Passover. The accusations have been repeated time and again and down the centuries, until the present day despite the fact that in the book of Leviticus, chapter 7 verse 26 there is an unambiguous commandment stating that, 'You shall eat no manner of blood.'

A year or so after we moved in full time to The Gables Jeremy announced that he wanted to keep ducks. I remembered our pair of mallards that we kept at The Old Forge 40 years ago. They lived in an enclosure in the corner of our small field and they were mucky and not very appealing in my eyes.

'I don't like ducks except in Regent's Park and I don't want ducks at The Gables,' I protested. Jeremy looked me in the eye and let out a deep and exasperated sigh.

'I knew you'd say that but I've found a breed that are so pretty even you will want them. And they're small and come in different colours. Before you say no just sit down and take a look at these.' He got out his phone and showed me some pictures and they looked cute and compact. 'Okay you win.' I reluctantly agreed to the purchase of two apricot-coloured call ducks, one female and one male, which we arranged to collect from a petting zoo outside Luton the following week. The ducks were living in a concrete enclosure, without any grass or natural water. They were quick to settle in at the smallholding where they had access to fresh air, grass and a pond. Call ducks are so named because hunters use them to 'call out' and attract other ducks when they go shooting. The females have a loud quack and the males are quieter but quite aggressive in the spring, often pushing the females under the water in the duck pond in their enthusiasm to mate. Our female was a prolific egg layer and then became a good nester and mother. Eventually we had 18 birds who wandered around the vegetable garden, helping us by snaffling up snails and slugs who wanted to eat our plants. At night we locked the birds away in a secure house. Then, one day, a canny vixen realised that if she bided her time in the daylight she could, two by two, pick off the ducks and take them home to her den and feed them to her hungry cubs. When we worked out what was happening we had no choice but to lock our ducks up in a run and put down organic slug pellets to protect our cabbages and brussels sprouts. As with our geese, subsequent ducks have not cared to sit on their nests and this year a silkie chicken sat on a baker's dozen of duck eggs. Ten ducklings hatched from this clutch and they and their surrogate mother are getting along beautifully. Quite soon the ducks will have their adult feathers and be able to join the older flock in the duck run. It seems that ducks, like geese, share a common language with chickens.

In December 2020 poultry breeders and keepers were issued with a notice from DEFRA – the Department for Environment, Food and Rural Affairs – requiring all hens, ducks and turkeys to be housed indoors to prevent the spread of a highly transmissible virus, avian influenza which had been killing wild fowl as well as commercially bred birds. We immediately relocated some of the chickens to the vacant quail barn and erected a polytunnel in one of the large chicken runs where we could keep the rest of the poultry. It was winter time and the hens seemed to enjoy the extra warmth of their new housing and instead of going off lay during the coldest months of the year, they continued to produce eggs almost daily. The order was not lifted until April 2021. The following November DEFRA again required all poultry to be incarcerated for a further six months and in November 2022 the birds were put inside for the third year in a row and only liberated at the end of April 2023. At the time of writing no vaccination against this virus and the only method used to stop the spread of the disease is by culling affected flocks and keeping poultry indoors away from wild birds who are said to be the culprits for infecting chickens and other commercial birds. As reported in The Guardian in December 2022, *'Globally, the disease – and related culling – has killed 140 million poultry since 2021, according to the World Organisation for Animal Health. This includes almost 48 million birds in Europe and the UK combined and just over 53 million in the US.'* An epidemiologist, Arjan Stegeman, at Utrecht University in the Netherlands says, *'If an industry can only remain by culling of animals it is not sustainable.'* Dan Crossley of the Food Ethics Council said, *'It is becoming almost normalised now that millions of birds are being culled, which is plain wrong.'*

Farmers in the UK receive compensation for any healthy birds who have to be killed after signs of avian flu appear in their flocks but this does not cover the costs of sick birds and the additional expenses of cleaning and disinfecting their vast sheds after the cull. Over the last year the rise in energy prices and animal feed has forced more and more poultry farmers out of the industry. This may be one of the problems. Chicken farming is considered an industry with the end consumers, some of us (not me, because I have been a vegetarian for over 50 years) having no idea or interest in how our food is raised and in what inhumane conditions. James Mottershead, the NFU poultry industry chair at the time of writing, operates six vast sheds that churn out 1.3 million chickens a year.

In May 2023 a High Court judge rejected a challenge brought by the animal rights charity Humane League UK which argued that fast growing chicken breeds suffer health and welfare problems. 90 per cent of the one billion chickens slaughtered and raised in this country have been genetically selected over decades to be fast-growing. They come to full weight in the extraordinarily short time of 35 days whereas in 1950 a broiler – hen raised for meat – would not be ready for slaughter until 84 days. Dr Marc Cooper of The Royal Society for the Protection of Animals – (RSPCA) – gave evidence in the case and said that the outcome represented, *'a significant failure to address the most pressing animal welfare issue of our time.'*

In contrast to the millions of birds raised in cramped conditions, with a short life of only five weeks, we keep less than 40 hens and know each of them by sight and by their nature. Some even have names. They produce eggs for us and our friends and family. They live until they die naturally. This is backyard egg production which is still practised throughout the world with some of the smallholders and farmers killing the occasional hen or rooster to cook in the pot or oven. The industrialisation of chicken farming takes away the dignity and individuality of the birds and desensitises the producer and the consumer who wants to eat cheap meat without a thought that their chicken burger was once a live creature kept with hundreds of thousands of other nameless creatures in a shed with restricted space. The culling process, too, is unimaginably cruel and not spoken of outside of those who have had the misfortune to witness the scene. Either carbon dioxide mixed with other inert gases is pumped into a sealed poultry shed or mobile gassing carts are used in a similar way so that the gas cannot escape. The birds fight for breath and then run out of oxygen and suffocate. Even when birds are NOT being culled because of avian flu but being slaughtered to go into the UK food chain the majority of chickens, hens and turkeys (according to the RSPCA) are now killed using gas. Placed in transport crates they are then exposed to the gas mixture and suffocate in situ avoiding (as the website states) *the need to handle and 'shackle' live birds, so has some welfare advantages!!!!* (my exclamation marks). The public should, in my opinion, also be aware that the other legal killing method in the UK is electrical, where birds are hung upside down by their legs on metal shackles and moved along a conveyor belt. They process along the production line to a stunning water bath and when the bird's head makes contact with the water, an electrical circuit between the water bath and shackle is completed, which stuns the birds. The conveyor belt then moves the birds to a mechanical neck cutter, which severs the major blood vessels in the neck. The RSPCA acknowledges that the shackling of live birds causes pain, and hanging birds by their legs is stressful for them.

At The Gables, when we have too many cockerels, I call a local friend. He dispatches the birds in situ, outdoors in the place where they have been hatched, raised and lived and nurtured for at least six months or a year alongside other birds, with daily access to grass, good and secure housing and plenty of food, corn and greens from the garden. Within moments he bashes the bird on the head with a piece of wood and then breaks their neck. I don't think the process even takes five seconds. The birds are then taken to his home where he plucks and dresses and eats them and shares any surplus meat with neighbours and family. Our friend says that they taste delicious and the bird, thoughtfully raised, enters the food chain with all involved understanding the process and the outcome.

The commodification of poultry extends to the bigger animals too namely cattle, pigs and sheep. The large-scale farming of these intelligent creatures ignores their need for a natural environment, interaction with other animals and individual care. As soon as these animals are ready to enter the food chain they are slaughtered in the following two-stage process. The first is stunning which causes the animal to lose consciousness and the second is the sticking when a very sharp knife is used to sever the blood vessels in its neck and chest.

Stunning can be carried out in one of three ways, all of which are controversial. The first is with a penetrating metal bolt which is fired into the brain of usually a cow or sheep and less often a pig. The first bolt does not always hit its mark and the process must be repeated on the terrified animal. The second is electrical and is used on sheep and calves and pigs where a current is passed through the animal's brain via a large pair of tongs causing a temporary loss of consciousness. The third is gas stunning and killing which is used on pigs and exposes them to high concentrations of gas causing the animal to suffocate from lack of oxygen and die in great distress.

After stunning, these large animals are shackled by a hind leg and hoisted above the ground and the slaughterer sticks the animal resulting in rapid blood loss and death. That is the reality of producing cheap meat for the consumer market and it hurts me to think not only of the deaths of these animals but, for far too many, the misery of their lives in an increasing number of mega farms.

The Gables is just a small patch of land compared with these industrial complexes yet we, like all farms and smallholdings, try to ensure that our animals are kept healthy and free from infection and disease. On a farm of any size there will always be a problem with keeping rodents away from the animal fodder. We wage a low-scale war against vermin and although the cats do their best to kill mice and shrews, they are not too keen on pursuing the rats. Nor am I, but the facts are that where there are ducks and hens and geese there will be rats. In the first years of our life here we were able to purchase rat poison online. Nowadays, quite correctly, the rules have been tightened and only customers with a registered farm or smallholding may buy the chemical and they must have a current rodent certificate. Initially Jeremy suggested I take the test, after the requisite amount of study, but I persuaded him that he was more likely to pass first time and he dutifully read the literature and took the online examination. On the mantelpiece is a framed certificate that proudly states that Jeremy has, 'successfully completed online training and assessment in Rodent Control on Farms.' With this proof he is allowed to buy the poison that keeps the rat population under control. Although I don't put out the poison or regulate its use I am quite prepared to sweep any dead rats into the large, long-handled scoop and later incinerate their bodies. Recently the rats were beginning to eat the food that we put out for the geese. Every morning when I went to check the food container it was completely empty. If I arrived there early I would see a rat or two running away as I approached the feeding bowl. Then they became bolder and barely minded me at all. From one or two there were suddenly five or six and then more. It was time to act against them and we moved the geese down to the pond and shut the gate to keep the flock away from their usual feeding station. Instead of a bowl of goose food Jeremy left out two dishes of rat poison. Gradually the dishes emptied and the rats got the message and left us alone. We might not be winning the war against rodents but we aren't losing either. Perhaps it is a stalemate which suits us all fine. We can share this place with a few rabbits, rodents and pigeons and accept the occasional loss of a goose taken by a fox but it's all about the balance and when it is people versus nature we have to give nature a chance.

CHAPTER THIRTEEN –
TO REMEMBER THE PAST AND LOOK TO THE FUTURE

As the evenings draw in and the clocks go back, when the Succah has been packed away and the wooden struts stored in the barn, it is time to turn to other matters both at The Gables and in the village. The last of the potatoes have to be dug up and stored in sacks before they are hit by the frosts. Green tomatoes on the vines will definitely not ripen as the days grow colder but they can be made into our daughter's favourite chutney. Jars of preserves are stored on the dresser shelves to be eaten here and also given away as gifts over the course of the winter and spring. This is the time to relish long evenings sitting in front of the warm wood-burning stove with one or both cats curled up on our laps.

Six years ago we received an email from the clerk of the Parish council. The minutes of the meeting, 4th October 2017, record that *'Councillor Pegler proposed that parishioners be invited to donate to a Silent Soldier rather than using public funds. The proposal was seconded and unanimously agreed. The clerk agreed to talk to the Royal British Legion about the best way to fund the soldier for gift aid and to talk to Highways about where to locate the soldier'.*

Following the Parish meeting everyone in the village received an email asking for donations towards the project. Within a couple of months £250 was raised. The Silent Soldier figurine, commemorating the fallen from World War I, was placed in the Colmworth Country Park adjacent to the Church and the cemetery. The statue would be in place in time to mark the centenary of the end of the First World War which was to be observed throughout Europe on 11th November 2018 and remains as a poignant reminder of all those men, some just teenage boys, who never returned to their waiting families.

On Remembrance Sunday in November the vicar of the Benefice holds a short service in the park. The Benefice is a group of churches sharing one minister and the vicar must rush from village to village to conduct Sunday services and, on Remembrance Sunday, to perform the commemoration in several locations.

There is a church in nearly every village on this island but the number of churchgoers is diminishing rapidly and the Church of England's own statistics in 2019 revealed that less than one per cent of the population attend a C of E church on a Sunday and a third of those 600,000 worshippers are over the age of 70. This is borne out in our village where the handful of people attending the weekly service are all pensioners. Heather used to organise a Christmas nativity which involved a few parents and children and an Easter egg hunt which was popular with families. The regular weekly services hardly ever attract any youngsters.

'At this rate,' Heather would sigh as we made our way along the footpaths on our regular Wednesday walk, 'There won't be anyone left to pay for the upkeep of the church. We already have difficulties with fixing a rota to clean the building or arrange fresh flowers. There are so few of us prepared to do anything and we are trying to run everything.'

'What about the building? I heard that you had to raise money to save the stained glass window and aren't there always roof repairs and wood rot in old churches?'

She sighed again. 'One of us has to spend hours and hours filling in forms to apply for grants. It's a never-ending battle.' Heather looked sad and weary. 'I just don't know what will become of the building and all the other ones like this.'

The situation was a source of great sadness to my friend, a deeply committed Christian who had served for many years as one of the church wardens and was a true believer in Christ. When she was in her last days I sat beside her, privileged to be able to hold her hand for a few precious minutes.

'You are going on an amazing journey.'

'Yes, I know,' she replied and she and I truly believed that to be so, each in our own way. I was excited for her although, selfishly, I was so very sad to be losing a dear and good friend.

The Church of St Denys in Colmworth is typical of so many places of worship. It is steeped in the history of England, with parts of the building dating back to the 15th century. I first entered the church on a

Sabbath afternoon walk that Jeremy and I took soon after we moved to The Gables ten years ago. Although I delight in the history of old church buildings and admire the jewelled colours of the windows and the artwork and artefacts on display, there is a part of me that recoils from entering because of the vicious antisemitism that was spread by the Church for many hundreds of years. Some Jews will not go inside a church at all and frown on those of us who will. The famous 12th century Rabbi and physician, Maimonides, the author of The Guide to the Perplexed and an early codifier of the laws of the Torah – the Old Testament – absolutely forbade Jews from entering Christian places of worship. His rationale was the biblical prohibition against Avoda Zora – idol worship – which he believed the worship of Jesus Christ to be. Additionally, the acknowledgement of the trinity of Father, Son and Holy Ghost further suggests that there are three divinities, not just one, which is problematic for Jews who only recognise a single deity.

Other rabbis, notably the 13th century Catalonian sage Rabbi Menachem HaMeiri, viewed Christians as, 'people whose lives are governed by religion,' and therefore the laws prohibiting idolatry or mixing with idol worshippers do not apply to Christians. There is an oft-spoken and very true phrase which states if there are, 'Two Jews in a room there will be three opinions.'

In 2022 Rabbi Mirvis, the Chief Rabbi of the United Hebrew Congregations of the Commonwealth, attended the platinum jubilee ceremony of Queen Elizabeth at Westminster Abbey. Following the death of the Queen, in May 2023 he was a guest at the coronation of King Charles which actually took place on the Sabbath. His dispensation came from the Rabbinical Court ruling of the London Beth Din – house of judgement – in 1970 which allows rabbis to attend Christian religious ceremonies only if the rabbi's presence is requested by the monarch. Some medieval scholars permitted court Jews, those close to the King, to violate certain prohibitions to ensure Jewish political safety. It's a contentious issue and many religious Jews who I know will indeed enter a church to admire its architecture or to honour a friend or neighbour at a funeral, to attend a wedding and less usually a christening of a baby. We tread a thin line and many of us come to our own conclusions whilst feeling that we may well be violating the rulings of rabbinic scholars of ages past and present.

Several times a year we invite different groups of friends and family to come and join us at The Gables to celebrate a festival or a Sabbath. Part of the programme will include, 'Gill's country walk' and very often our guests will ask, 'Can we go to the village?' I warn them that, 'We can go on the road or through the fields. But either way when we get to the village don't be disappointed. There is nothing much to see there because there isn't a pub or a village green or a shop or a post office. The only place of interest is the church.'

'Can we take a look in the church? Is it open?'

'It's usually open. They decided to lock it a few years ago and we could only go in by arrangement. That didn't last for long but it's still shut at night and one evening, some kids drilled a hole in the old wooden door to get inside. All they found was a tin of biscuits but it took months and months for the insurance company to process the claim. The church still had to pay an excess of several hundred pounds to repair the hole in the oak door. There really isn't much else that the wardens and the vicars can do to keep vandals at bay.'

'I've heard that thieves strip lead from church roofs and that costs a fortune to replace. It's so sad,' Gila once said to me after our Sabbath group had walked to the village. We didn't know it then, but her words proved to be prophetic. The roof of the nearby church in Keysoe was vandalised a few years ago and all the lead removed and probably sold as scrap.

Inside the church, after my friends have wandered around and looked at the building, I always ask everyone to come to the front and gather around the Dyer monument which stands inside the north wall by the altar and has a fascinating, upsetting and overwhelmingly romantic history.

Katherine Doyley was born to an aristocratic landowner father, John Doyley of Merton in 1585 and in 1602 she married Sir William Dyer of Great Staughton, Bedfordshire when she was 17 or 18. Their marriage was blessed with seven children. In 1621 Sir William died leaving his young widow to bring up the family on her own and in 1641 Lady Katherine erected a finely carved alabaster and black marble monument in the church of St Denys, Colmworth to memorialise her late husband. Beneath the effigy of a supine Sir William is one of his widow Lady Dyer and below that on the panelled base are carved the figures of Faith, Hope and Charity. Between these three sculptures stand the carvings of the four Dyer sons and the three daughters. Two of the boys wear the clothing associated with Oliver Cromwell's Roundheads and two are dressed as Royalists. The daughters all hold large handkerchiefs in their hands and appear to be crying. This split in the family loyalties is depicted for all to see on the monument and must have been heartbreaking for Lady Katherine and her daughters as they lived through the turbulent years of the English Civil War. Above the figure of Sir William is inscribed the romantic poem written by Lady Katherine, entitled 'My Dearest Dust.' It is full of longing and grief and is the very first known documented poem by an English woman. It can still be found in many anthologies of English verse.

Some years ago I wrote to John Julius Norwich asking for financial assistance to maintain St Denys Church. I was a member of a group of non-church going locals called the 'Friends of St Denys', who were trying to raise funds for the costs of caring for the historic building. Although Viscount Norwich (who died on June 1st 2018) was unable to become involved with the fund raising he sent a donation in recognition of the importance of Lady Katherine's poem in the canon of English literature. I usually ask one of my visitors to read the poem out loud. The lines quoted below are from the second and better known of the two verses.

'My dearest dust, could not thy hasty day
Afford thy drowzy patience leave to stay
One hower longer: so that we might either
Sate up, or gone to bedd together?
Thy weary limbs with early rest
Enjoy it sweetly and thy widdowe bride
Shall soone repose her by thy slumbring side
Whose business, now, is only to prepare
My nightly dress, and call to prayer
Mine eyes wax heavy and ye day growes old
The dew falls thick, my beloved growes cold
Draw, draw ye closed curtaynes: and make room:
My dear, my dearest dust, I come, I come'

Lady Katherine never remarried and died in in 1654 at the age of 69. In her will she mentioned, 'her losses had become very great since those last trouble,' of the Civil War. One of the Dyer children, Ann, married a Gery of Bushmeade Priory which is about a mile north of St Denys Church on the road to Little Staughton. There are descendants of the family still living in the area and in charge of the ancient Priory which can only be visited by appointment with The English Heritage Trust. The Priory is a rare survival of an Augustinian refectory with 14th century wall paintings. The past is always present.

There is another historic and close connection between the village of Colmworth and the founders of the Mormon Church in America. During one of our chats when Heather and I would sit drinking tea in her conservatory, she told me that, 'Over the years I've seen strangers taking photographs in and around the church. When I stopped and asked them who they were many of them turned out to be Americans looking for the grave of Reverend Matthews.'

'Why were they interested in the Reverend Timothy Matthews? I've seen his grave, it's bigger than anyone else's and I've read a bit about him but I don't understand.'

'It's a long story and I can't remember all the details. I know you like to look stuff up on Google so why don't you do that when you go home and we'll discuss it again next time we meet.'

I did indeed Google the Reverend Timothy Matthews and found quite a few sources of information about the man, whose trademark bugle is engraved on his tomb.

Timothy Matthews was born in Lincolnshire in 1795 and ordained as an Anglican clergyman serving as a curate both at nearby Bolnhurst Church and also at St Denys Church between 1818 and 1830. He was known to be a fine preacher but also a highly controversial figure and a law unto himself, more often than not at odds with the established Anglican Church and its bishops. In contravention of their wishes he regularly preached at nonconformist places of worship and after a bitter confrontation with his bishop, Matthews became a street preacher parading through Bedford blowing a bugle to summon people to his side. On a Sunday in 1841 he was reputed to have personally baptised over 2000 new converts in one day, dipping them in the waters of the Great River Ouse beside Bedford Town bridge. That must have been quite a sight. His new converts and followers tried to raise money to build Reverend Matthews his own chapel but he died in Bedford in 1845 before sufficient funds had been collected. He was buried in unconsecrated ground at the Bromham Road church where he preached and his body was later moved to the churchyard in Colmworth where his grave can be seen (and photographed) to this day on the north side of the churchyard.

Reverend Matthews married Ann Fielding in 1821. Her family had moved from Halifax to farm some land in Staploe, Bedfordshire and Ann was born in the hamlet of Honeydon which adjoins Colmworth and is, coincidentally, also where my friend Heather lived. Ann was one of six Fielding children. Her sister Mary, the youngest, was born in 1801 and in 1834 Mary emigrated to Toronto, Canada to join two of her older siblings, Joseph Fielding and Mercy Fielding. Joseph and Mercy and Mary were introduced to the Church of the Latter Day Saints in 1836 by a family friend John Taylor at a religious study group in Toronto. Two years later all three Fieldings moved to Ohio to join the larger body of their Church and in 1837 the recently bereaved Hyrum Smith (one of the leaders of the Latter Day Saints) courted Mary and they married in 1837 with Mary bringing up the widower's children as well as her own son and daughter. After Hyrum Smith and his brother Joseph Smith were killed and martyred for their faith, Mary fled with the rest of the Latter Day Saints from Illinois to Utah, making the Long Trek of 1,300 gruelling miles by wagon and on foot. It was a terrible and arduous journey with many of the adherents of the faith dying along the way and suffering great hardships even when they arrived in Utah. Mary settled with her children in their adopted home and she died in 1852 at the age of 51 and is buried in Salt Lake City. Mary Fielding, a girl from the hamlet of Honeydon, adjacent to Colmworth, became one of America's great pioneers. The wife of one Mormon leader, Hyrum Smith, the mother of another (her son Joseph became the sixth President of the Church in 1901) and the grandmother of another who became the tenth President of the Church in 1970. I find this quite extraordinary. From Bedfordshire to Utah, from St Denys Church to the Church of the Latter Day Saints. That is quite a journey both physically and spiritually and I marvel at the courage that this woman possessed. She not only left her family behind in England but travelled to Canada, America and finally to the state of Utah knowing that it would be unlikely that she would ever return to Honeydon and see her parents again. The past is always present, especially in Colmworth churchyard.

Four years ago I received a telephone call from a member of the church. 'Gill,' she said, 'The Reverend Tim asked me to call you. We would really like you to take part in the Remembrance Service as a member of the Jewish community. Do you think you could recite a suitable prayer?'

'May I have a day or two to think about it and consult with Jeremy?'

'Of course.'

I telephoned her the next day. 'I'd be honoured to take part and please thank the vicar for asking me.'

Jeremy showed me the Hebrew Kal Maale Rachamim – God full of Mercy – verses in our daily prayer book. This is a memorial prayer and a version had been adapted to commemorate the fallen soldiers of both World Wars and other conflicts. The prayer ends with a request that these departed souls find 'eternal rest under the wings of the divine presence.'

For the three weeks leading up to Remembrance Sunday I practised singing the prayer out loud. On the appointed morning I was nervous and hoped that I would acquit myself well not only for my own sake but because I felt that I was representing my tribe in my adopted, thoroughly English village. I had been to the service in previous years but this time, with a new vicar in place, he was making an effort to include other faiths and I didn't want to let him or myself down. The vicar's readings were short, the wreath-laying by the Chair of the Parish council and a representative of St Denys Church was dignified. A village resident, a member of the Territorial Army, spoke the moving words, 'They shall not grow old as we that are left grow old,' from the poem 'For the Fallen' written by Laurence Binyon and published in The Times in 1914. After this the bugler in his Salvation Army uniform played the Last Post and Reveille. Our friend, in his mellifluous American voice, recited by heart, 'In Flanders Fields', the now famous poem written in 1915 by a Canadian doctor Lieutenant John McCrae after he lost a friend in Ypres. I sang, in Hebrew, the Kal Maale Rachamim and then read out an English translation. Then we all stood in silence for two minutes and the final notes were sounded. After a reading from the Old Testament and a short address from the vicar we recited The Lord's Prayer and then sang 'God save the Queen'.

It was an emotional morning as I remembered, as I always do, my Grandpa Sam – my father's father and the tragic story connected to his wife, my Grandma Katy. I continued to think of them as I drove home and for the rest of that day.

My father's parents were both born in Odessa, Grandpa Sam in 1897 and Grandma Katy in 1898 and they immigrated to this country with their parents and siblings in 1901. Like so many immigrants before them and after, they were escaping poverty and persecution but unlike many other refugees they were also fleeing from anti-Jewish pogroms which began in Odessa in 1821 and took place again in 1859, 1871 and more frequently and violently from 1881, when Tsar Alexander II was murdered by revolutionaries. Following the assassination of the Tsar the Russian government enacted the May Laws which seriously restricted Jewish rights of trade and residence and education and which encouraged (with tacit government approval) more and more anti-Jewish riots. Further draconian laws followed in 1887 and 1891 and in the subsequent 30 years over 2,000,000 Jews left the Russian Empire with most travelling to America but over 100,000 settling in Great Britain, the vast majority not far from the docks in the crowded streets of the East End of London. In 1905 the Pogrom of Odessa resulted in the death of over 400 Jews and the destruction and damage of over 1600 Jewish properties. Thankfully my great grandparents had the foresight and opportunity to leave the city of their birth before those terrible events. Tragically they had friends and relatives left behind in Odessa who were affected by the violence and bloodshed.

My family would have been typical of the thousands of Jewish immigrants arriving on these shores. The adults spoke Yiddish not English. Their children would grow up speaking both. Most of these new arrivals had spent what little money they had on the journey and when they set foot on land their immediate need was for food, shelter and work. The 60,000 Jews who were already settled in England by the end of the 19th century were not delighted to be faced with the 'immigrant problem' of their co-religionists. Fortunately, some rose to the challenge establishing the Poor Jews Temporary Shelter in Leman Street in 1885 and a soup kitchen in Brick Lane, both near the docks. The Board of Guardians of the Jewish Poor was set up by some of the

English upper-class Jewish establishment in 1859. The aim of the Board was to help the Jewish poor mainly by giving loans to those with the greatest need. The more settled and wealthier Jews in England, including many members of the Rothschild banking family, were approached for donations and it was their money which sustained the activities of the Board although they were unable to cover all the needs of the Jewish poor. The Board had strict criteria and new immigrants could not apply for relief until they had been in the country for six months. This rule was an attempt to discourage mass immigration of poor Jews from Russia and Eastern Europe but once they had arrived the Board took on the responsibility of doing what they could to help the individuals and their families making exceptions to the six month residency rule for those who were ill or elderly. Between 1900 and 1910 the Board of Guardians made over 26,000 financial payments to East End Jews averaging £7 per loan. These were interest-free and were used to buy sewing machines for tailors, tools for carpenters and cabinet makers, machinery for book binders and printers and cobblers, all of which would enable the recipients to earn a living and support themselves and to repay the loan over a period of time.

My grandma Katy's family was typical of many of these poor immigrants.

Nearly 30 years ago Jeremy and I visited Grandma's 92 year old sister, Jenny, who was living in a Jewish care home in South London. Her memory and recall of the immigrant life in London was crystal clear and later she wrote us a letter outlining all that she could remember of the family and their living conditions in the East End.

'What can I tell you about our 'ancestors'? Not much, I only know the Russian version what my mother told me. Her father had a butcher shop. Mother had four brothers and they all emigrated to America. Father's mother had a small factory in Odessa that employed young girls to make ladies underwear. They wore calico in those days and my mother was one of the girls. I don't know about the romance of my father and mother, all I do know is that they lived and married in Odessa and had four children, Sarah, Harry, Katy and Samuel. Father was a cigarette maker which was not very lucrative, it was hard work with poor pay. His employer opened a factory in Glasgow. It wasn't successful so he came to London and opened another cigarette factory and my father and others came to London to work for him. So the Russian period ended.

Starting with London, after a lot of difficulty, the family found a flat in Brunswick Building, Aldgate, my birthplace, the top floor about 100 or more stairs. I am not sure because I don't remember living there. I do remember living in Dunstan Houses, Stepney Green. I don't remember Tony being born but I do remember Abe because, if I am not mistaken, one of the neighbours took me for a walk because mother was giving birth upstairs to Abe. I was a young child then and children didn't know much about life. Everything was a secret. We weren't told and we were not allowed to ask questions. I know we lived in Dunstan Houses for some years but most of my memories are of 36 Cressy Place, a small two up and two down where we were all raised.

Father, Sarah, Katy and myself were cigarette makers and we learned the trade at home because father had to do work at night as well as at his employers to make ends meet. We all had to 'chip in' and do our share, the boys too were taught to do their bit. Life was hard, money scarce and we struggled along. No hundreds of pounds a week then, wages were counted in shillings. The modern young person doesn't know hardship, thank goodness.'

Jenny's letter goes on to describe the spouses of each of her six siblings and their families. Her letter concludes as follows,

'All the others married and had children but I am the only one who married late in life because I looked after my mother who became bedridden and blind, so I didn't marry until my mother died in 1948.'

Katy's husband, my Grandpa Sam, came from a traditional religious family and his father worked as a tailor. The six brothers and sisters lived in a four-room slum house, just like so many thousands of others. When the First World War began and there was a drive to recruit soldiers Grandpa Sam signed up even though he was underage. He probably thought that this would be an adventure with the opportunity of going abroad as well as a chance to earn a regular wage. No longer would he have to share a room and bed with his siblings. As we now know, most of the recruits had a wretched time at the front and spent weeks or months living in muddy trenches, with inadequate food, no sanitation and constantly at risk of disease, injury and death. Grandpa was at the infamous Battle of the Somme. He used to tell my younger brother how, 'We slept in the trenches with rats running over us. I still wake up here, in my bed, having nightmares about it.'

He didn't say much more to either of us about his war and, like many thousands of others, he kept the horrors as well as some of the adventures well hidden. These soldiers rarely received a hero's welcome on their return to civilian life nor were they given, as they would be today, any counselling or recognition of their trauma. They didn't talk about their experiences and their families didn't question them.

Fifteen years ago, when my dad Leslie, Sam's only son, was conducting a regular and intimate email correspondence with our son he sent this description of Grandpa Sam's war.

'My dad left home in 1914 and enlisted in the Royal Artillery. I suppose that my grandparents and their contemporaries must have been made of stern stuff as they did not worry unduly about their sons who had gone off to war. Perhaps I'm wrong to make such an assumption but then there's no one left whom I can ask. Obviously that generation were made in a different mould. They had the courage and determination to travel far away to a strange country where they could not speak the language and where the prospects were unknown. They must have been sustained by a deep faith in God. I think that I have not inherited their genes for I, unlike them, am a terrible pessimist and I could worry for England. I suppose that as they had to work long hours to earn sufficient to feed a family they did not have the luxury of having time for worries about their many children. Back to my dad. From what I can remember he was the only Jew in his battalion. I suppose that his comrades had never before met a Jew. He was taught how to care for a horse as he was in a unit that had horses that pulled gun carriages. Apart from grooming he had to muck out and learn all the tricks of the trade. He told me that he could ride bareback as the animal pulled along the cannon. His stories of conditions in the trenches were horrifying. The fields and trenches were knee deep in mud and duckboards were used to enable the troops to walk. There were hair-raising stories of rats and fleas and terrible food. It was a war of attrition and he took part in many battles where there were large numbers of casualties suffered to gain a few hundred yards of territory only for more casualties to be suffered when the Germans counterattacked and regained the recently won ground. Apart from his awful experiences he had many good times when he was on leave as he was very much a ladies' man and the French girls were partial to British Tommies. He sprinkled his reminiscences with names such as Abbeville, Lille and Ypres the latter being pronounced in the way the Tommies did – Wipers. He spoke of the Battle of the Somme and of the time that he was going into the line when he met his eldest brother who was leaving the line. Their respective commanding officers gave them permission to spend a day together. Fortunately both the brothers survived and returned home after the War. My father often spoke about how many

dead bodies he had seen and told me that was why he wasn't afraid of death having had so many near death experiences. After The Armistice, because he spoke fluent Yiddish which to all intents and purposes was German, he was assigned to a Prisoner of War Camp. He told me that the behaviour of the British soldiers was as brutal and as bestial as the purported behaviour of the Germans in Belgium at the outset of the conflict. It always puzzled me as a child how God knew to whom victory should go as I thought that Jewish Englishmen were praying to him for an Allied victory and Jewish Germans were praying for a similar outcome. I wonder what criteria was used to resolve such a dilemma. Anyway to return to my Pop. After he was demobbed he became a porter in the morgue of the London Jewish Hospital. He told me that he could do that job easily because having seen so many dead soldiers he was no longer squeamish.'

Grandma Katy had her own First World War story and every day I look at the two pictures that hang just above my desk and think of her and the soldier.

100,000 troops and nurses, out of a population of just over a million people, left New Zealand for service overseas when the war began in 1914. Most of the troops were sent to Northern France to fight on the Western Front which stretched from Belgium to France although some were sent to Samoa, Gallipoli and Sinai-Palestine. In London, at a dance, Grandma Katy made the acquaintance of a young New Zealand soldier, who was thousands of miles away from home waiting to cross the channel to fight for King and country. I don't know how much time they had together, maybe days or a week or two at most. Grandma learnt that the young man was a farmer's son who lived on a large sheep farm back in New Zealand and before the soldier left Grandma gave him her address. She always told me that she was going to marry him and maybe she would have done so except that Katy was scared of animals, the soldier wasn't Jewish and I doubt that Grandma had any idea about the life of a sheep farmer in New Zealand. The soldier sent Grandma hand-embroidered cards from, 'Somewhere in France.' The troops were not allowed to divulge their location even to their loved ones. The card above my desk has, written in golden silk thread, the words, 'Heaps of kisses for my darling.' A second card is decorated with purple and yellow flowers above the line, 'To my dear girl'. The soldier never returned and I always hoped that writing to Katy, believing that the girl he met on the way to the front would one day be his bride, gave this poor lad some comfort in his short life.

Over 16,000 of the New Zealand troops lost their lives in the conflict and 40,000 were injured. Many New Zealanders fought and died at The Battle of the Somme where, ironically, Grandpa Sam was one of the lucky British survivors. Whenever I glance up at those cards I feel indescribably sad both for Katy, who was never truly happy in her marriage to Sam, for Sam who was disappointed in his marriage with Katy and above all for the young soldier whose life was ended so cruelly, so very far from home and whose name I never knew.

In her old age Grandma Katy went out every day riding the buses for free with her bus pass while Grandpa Sam sat in his armchair smoking his Senior Service tipped cigarettes and putting small each-way bets on the horse racing that he watched all afternoon on the television. Some days he was lucky, other days he lost his money. Overall, he was neither a winner nor a loser on the horses or in life.

Grandpa might have been pleased to know that Huntingdon Race Course is just 20 minutes north of our village. Jeremy and I last visited the track on a sunny Boxing Day in 2022 arriving just in time to lay a bet with the bookies a minute before the first race. The afternoon started well for me with a winner and a handful of change and notes to stake on subsequent races. I lost the lot and more besides but it was a great day out watching not only the graceful horses and their colourful silk-clad jockeys but also the eclectic crowd. There were families pushing babies in buggies and toddlers sitting on their fathers' shoulders. Groups of young bucks and their girls, dressed to the nines in short skirts and high heels, gathered together to drink and laugh and party in the sunshine. Some, like us, were in warm, sensible attire with comfortable shoes. It was just as well because the stands were packed and even on the rails I had to jostle to find a space. It was full everywhere, with good-natured queues for the ladies toilets almost around the block. Drinkers spilled out of the bars and the food kiosks did a roaring trade. Lines formed at the Tote window and down by the track some collected their winnings from the turf accountants and others stood waiting to place their bets. The boards showed the name of each bookie and as the money was placed the odds on the horses changed. The prices were shown in lights visible from several feet away and we scanned the boards looking to see which horses were the favourites and which were outsiders. In between races we rushed to the ring to look at the steeds being led around by their stable lasses and lads.

'I like the look of that one. What's the name?'

We consulted our racing card and read the form on each horse before placing our bets. I was impatient and keen to get back to the bookies.

'Who are you going to back?' I asked Jeremy.

'I don't know yet, let me read about that one over there.' As with everything Jeremy wanted to consider his options thoroughly and I just wanted to put my bet on without any research.

'Let's bet on different horses. That makes the race more fun. Please don't take too long deciding,' I implored him. 'We don't want to miss the start.'

There was no rhyme or reason to my selections. Sometimes the horse had a ribbon woven into its mane that caught my eye or a name that sounded lucky. Just in time, we ran back to place our bets and then muscled into spaces that didn't really exist to get ready for the race. Stewards in hi-vis jackets tried to keep a gangway clear in the stands but as fast as they shooed us, the punters, away from the steps, we drifted back and the pathway disappeared under the swell of thousands of excited racegoers. It was, as we later discovered, the very last Boxing Day meeting to be held at Huntingdon and the day had a carnival air.

The previous time we had been to Huntingdon a friend from London had invited us along to watch his nag in one of the early races. The start was delayed for a health and safety issue and after three false attempts they were under starter's orders and then off and running but Harold's horse decided to walk backwards whilst all the other riders set off in the other direction at a furious gallop. I had to stifle my giggles as I looked at the mortified expression on Harold's face. The trainer told us that the horse had, 'psychological problems as a result of previous trauma.' Maybe it got some counselling but I don't think it ever raced again.

Back in January 2015 Harold had invited us to watch his horse, Iron Butterfly run at Huntingdon. This was my first outing to the racetrack since moving to The Gables.

'May we bring our friend Kate? She's mad about horses and she's ridden all her life. I haven't mentioned anything to her but I'm sure she'd like to come too.'

'Of course, the more the merrier. I'll have a friend with me and we can all have a drink together and stand in the owner's enclosure before the race.'

We met up inside the ground and wandered over to the ring where the four of us stood on the grass inside the circular cinder path, waiting for Iron Butterfly, to appear. The horse was glossy and slim with a plaited mane and tail and was led by an equally well-turned-out stable girl. All the steeds were beautiful and groomed to perfection. The jockeys, small and wiry, each wore the individual colours of the owners for whom they were riding in that race. The sun shone down as we set off for the stands and found a good viewing position. Within two minutes they were under starters orders and they were off. Cameras followed the field and on large screens we could see the horses as they rounded the bend. As they came into view I was yelling, 'Come on Iron Butterfly, come on my beauty. Come on, come on.'

My adrenaline was pumping as I watched the horses and jockeys flying past for the final lap of the course. As they galloped towards the finishing line the gap widened between the winners and the rest of the field and, sadly, Harold's horse didn't make the first three. Those holding winning betting slips were beaming whilst the rest of us threw our tickets away and began studying form determined to pick a winner next time. We stayed on for another race but, as it was a Friday afternoon, we needed to get home in good time so that I could heat the food for the oncoming Sabbath, feed and lock up the animals, have a bath and change into my Sabbath clothes. Harold and his travelling companion also needed to return to London promptly so we all set off before the last three races. 'Thanks for inviting us. Sorry that your horse didn't win.'

'That's okay, the trainer didn't expect anything. It was just good experience for him.'

'Bye. Shabbat shalom.'

'Shabbat shalom. He'll do better next time.'

Kate, Jeremy and I got into our car and turned on the radio. Two days earlier, on the 7th of January, France and much of the world had been shaken by the killings and injuries inflicted on journalists, police and bystanders at the Paris offices of the satirical magazine, Charlie Hebdo. Two French brothers, Muslim terrorists, carried out the attack in response to the publication of a cartoon of the Prophet, peace be upon him, which they believed to be blasphemous.

As we listened to the BBC News we were horrified to hear of another developing hostage situation and possible killings taking place at a Hypercacher kosher food supermarket in east Paris. I felt sick. Like me, these Jews in the suburbs of Paris were preparing for the day of rest. They were buying food and wishing each other 'Shabbat Shalom' as they went in and out of their local shop, anticipating a peaceful and pleasant Friday night family dinner. Kate didn't try to talk to either of us as we drove home. When we reached our road she said, 'Just drop me here. I'll speak to you another time. Sorry about what's going on but thank you for taking me with you.'

'Bye Kate, I'll call you on Sunday. Sorry.'

Our Sabbath had to be organised even though I had a heavy heart. The rules of the Sabbath may only be broken for the sake of saving a life. What we did in Colmworth would have no bearing on what was happening in Paris.

I heated the food and put dishes of rice and potatoes, lentils and vegetables onto the electric hot plate to keep them warm. The table had been laid earlier in the morning with a white cloth, our best china, glasses, cutlery and white serviettes. The silver kiddush cup over which Jeremy would make the blessing for wine before the meal stood next to the wooden bread board and silver knife with which he would cut the two loaves of chollahs – the plaited Sabbath bread. A pair of candles in glass candlesticks stood on a tray ready to be lit and blessed to 'usher in' the 25 hours of the Sabbath which would, in normal circumstances, be peaceful and relaxing. On this Friday, with the radio and television switched on until minutes before I struck the match to light the wicks, life did not feel peaceful. Jews were under attack as revenge for, the gunman was recorded as saying, 'the Western coalition actions in Mali, Iraq and Afghanistan and the Syrian government's actions.'

We went into that Sabbath unaware that four people had died, others had been injured and many traumatised.

What we did know, and what our daughter later wrote in the first report on antisemitism presented by her colleague at the United Nations in 2019, was that throughout the world wherever Jews live and even when their community is only counted in hundreds, every Jewish school and every Jewish place of worship has guards at its gates. Our children grow up in institutions where security at the entrance door is a given and where they and we do not even question its existence. With just fifteen million Jews in the whole world out of a population of 7 billion souls, why is it that every Jewish nursery school, junior school, high school and synagogue has to be guarded? Are we really such a threat and do we really inspire such fear and loathing that we must daily guard ourselves and our children against attack and death?

CHAPTER FOURTEEN –
LIGHT IN THE DARKNESS

'Won't you feel cut off in the winter time?' asked my brother.

'Not at all. I'll be happy to have some time without visitors. There are things I want to try, like spinning and crocheting. I want to catch up with films and documentaries on TV and do lots and lots of reading.'

By the time November had come and gone and we had tidied up the garden, put away the tools and stored the potatoes and squashes, we were ready to spend long evenings in our easy chairs enjoying the warmth of the wood burner usually with a glass of whisky in our hands. Every morning the first one up took out the wood ash and filled up the large, rush baskets with kindling and logs ready for relighting the fire.

The well-seasoned wood arrived in September in a tipper truck and was unloaded on the drive. There followed an hour piling the logs into wheelbarrows, pushing them to the woodshed and stacking them. Actually, we threw the wood onto a pile which would have shocked and appalled my Swedish friend, Marianne. Three years ago for my birthday she sent me a copy of the best selling book Norwegian Wood: Chopping, Stacking and Drying Wood the Scandinavian Way. Our woodpile looked nothing like any of the artistic and neat pictures on the pages and I hoped that Marianne would never ask me to send her a photograph of our endeavours.

In the winter the animals are content to stay indoors until the sun rises which gives us extra time in bed. In the summertime the dawn arrives, the cockerels begin to crow and we get up early and are often working outside until 8 pm or later, taking advantage of the evening light to plant and sow and weed and harvest. Our routines follow the pattern of the seasons and the daylight hours. When I lived in London I wasn't in tune with these differences. I drove to work in the dark in the winter and came home the same way but I didn't alter my hours. Summer or winter did not affect my lifestyle or my activities. That changed when I moved to The Gables.

In Devon, back in 1978, when we relocated from the hubbub of inner-city London, it took me a while to get used to the dark and quiet nights. It was rare for a car to drive past our cottage in the evening and during the day the only regular traffic was the rumble of the milk tanker on its way to collect and return from the many outlying dairy farms, the postman in his trademark red van, the milkman and the school bus. In the Devon winters I spent evenings by the fire with a basket of wool at my feet and a pair of carders in my hands, preparing fleeces for spinning by brushing them and removing the tangles. When I had enough carded wool I would get out my spinning wheel and begin the process of turning the fluffy balls into skeins ready for knitting. Jacob sheep have black and white fleeces and no two sheep are the same. The wool varies in colour and texture and the jumpers and cardigans that we and our baby son wore were as individual as the sheep. Forty years ago Jacob fleeces were prized and sought after by hobby spinners who sold their home-made garments at craft fairs around the county.

One year, in the Market House pub in Crediton where all the local hippies gathered to drink, we met two shaggy-haired New Zealanders. They were working their way across Europe by shearing sheep on farms and occasionally for smallholders like us.

'If we drive you to our place and give you supper and a couple of pounds would you shear our two Jacob ewes?'

'Why not. You've got a deal.'

The strong young men carried the ewes from the field into our garden where they quickly removed the fleeces, rolled and tied them and carried the shorn girls back to the pasture. Back home in New Zealand they were used to a back-breaking day working on huge farms that raised thousands of sheep. Gangs of shearers would stay at these isolated spreads and work for days until all the sheep were shorn. Our two placid ewes were a 'piece of .....' as they put it in the vernacular. After supper we drove them back into town where we drank pints of strong scrumpy at the pub before we headed home and they bedded down in a cheap room at the hostelry.

Forty years later sheep are still shorn by hand. It's a skilled job that is hard on the back and legs and our local shearer gave up the task a few years ago when he spent nearly as much as he earned from shearing on treatment at the osteopath. Three years ago I found a young woman online who told me, 'I haven't got an address. I live in my van with my dog and I'll go wherever I find work.' We arranged a date and she arrived in her vehicle with her beautiful sheepdog sitting up front in the passenger seat. Rachel was as good as her word and she was fast, efficient and extremely personable. Jeremy and I talked with her as she worked and found out that she spent the winters shearing abroad, 'Obviously there's no work here during the cold months but I get by and it gives me a chance to see other places. I might even fall in love with a foreign farmer!' As we continued to talk I realised that she actually had a beau abroad but he and his family raised cattle and her passion was sheep. She would have to make a decision as to where she settled and with which animals as well as with which man!

The following year Rachel returned to us and sheared the flock.

'May I pass your name to my neighbour? Two of them have small flocks like us and everyone's always looking for shearers. There aren't many around here because this is arable country, crops not cows or sheep.'

'With pleasure, I'd be pleased to look after them.'

A month later I got a WhatsApp from Rachel. She apologised as she could no longer help our neighbours with their sheep. Her van had been stolen when she was staying in a friend's house and all her equipment had gone with the vehicle. That was her livelihood, the tools of her trade. Thankfully her dog was indoors with her otherwise the thieves might have taken him. Trained sheepdogs are valuable with a good one costing more than £2000 and the bond between animal and master is deep and personal.

This year when I messaged Rachel there was no reply but her status photograph showed her with her dog against a backdrop of fir trees and a herd of cows. I think I know where she is and the decision she made. I wish her luck.

Our local farmer recommended another young woman, Katie, a freelance shepherdess with plenty of experience with sheep who trained on a course run by the British Wool Marketing Board which offers 800 places a year to would-be shearers. Katie told me, 'All the courses are really popular and they always fill the places, which are limited.

Afterwards you have to get lots of shearing jobs to put into practice what you learn.'

Because of daytime commitments Katie could only visit us on a weekday evening. We pencilled in a Tuesday so long as the weather held. Fleeces need to be dry to be cut otherwise the wool is heavy, the sheep weighed down and the stored wool will become mouldy and unusable. If the sheep is wet both shearer and sheep run the risk of slipping on the wooden shearing board and handlers can develop infections and boils if they are working with damp animals. Luckily for us, this year, the weather was dry and Katie arrived with her board and razor, three beautiful and friendly sheepdogs and a big smile and a great deal of energy. She was a skilled operator. We brought the girls and Tufty inside the barn and Jeremy passed the sheep out to Katie, one by one. She upended the sheep onto the wooden platform with a single move and manoeuvred the animal deftly to reach back, front, sides and tail without any assistance from either of us. There wasn't a drop of blood spilled in the two hours of cutting and shearing, which is truly rare. Wriggling sheep are often nicked and the cuts need to be treated with a squirt of antibacterial spray before the animal is let out into the field again.

'When you get home will your mum have made you something to eat?'

'Yes, she will and I'm starving. I've been at work since 8 o'clock this morning and I won't sit down until 9 o'clock tonight.'

'We're very grateful. You've done a fantastic job. Thank you and let's hope you can fit us in again next year.'

According to the International Wool Textile Organisation there is archaeological evidence of wool gathering and spinning as far back as 6000 BCE. A piece of European wool textile was found preserved in a Danish bog which dates back to 1500 BCE. In Britain cloth was being woven in the Bronze Age with shearing dating back to the Iron Age. By the time that the Romans arrived in Britain in 55 BCE there was a wool industry producing woven cloth. In 50 CE the Romans established a wool plant in Winchester to develop the methods of the British weavers. By the 8th century Britain was exporting woollen fabrics to the continent and this trade grew after the Norman Conquest in 1066. Wool, its production, cloth manufacture and trade both at home and on the continent was the backbone of the Medieval English economy. Until 2006 the seat of the Lord Chancellor in the House of Lords was a large square bag of wool called The Woolsack and since 2006 The Woolsack has been the seat of the Lord Speaker in that house, reminding us that wool was the principal source of English wealth in the Middle Ages. Up and down the land huge numbers of sheep were raised for their wool and their fleeces were prized by the finest Flemish weavers, many of whom came to settle and trade in England. By 1290 it is estimated that there were 5,000,000 sheep in England producing 30,000 sacks of wool a year.

Wool, cloth production and its export remained an important part of the economy and grew during the Industrial Revolution when Leeds and Bradford and their environs became the centres of mechanised mills which produced and exported woollen textiles all over the world. The mills required huge quantities of fleeces and these were not only supplied at home but from the growing sheep farms in the colonies of New Zealand and Australia. By the early 1960s the English mills were threatened with increasing imports of cheap cloth from the Far East and later from man-made material. Today nearly all of the Victorian edifices have closed with most redeveloped as luxury flats and some of the buildings demolished.

A disproportionate number of the textile mills were established and run by Jewish immigrants. Many arrived from Germany in the mid 19th century and a whole area of Bradford became known as Little Germany. Some of these entrepreneurs had brought their skills with them from the continent but others, as an article in the Yorkshire Observer stated in 1934, *'Knew very little about the manufacturing side of the industry, but they allied their powers as salesmen to the prowess of their Yorkshire colleagues as craftsmen and between the two of them Bradford captured the markets of the world.'*

One of Jeremy's great aunts married a man whose family established a mill in Shipley near Bradford. His family, the Jeromes, were escaping the so called Irish Pogrom in Limerick and left Ireland in 1904. It's a tragic story of antisemitism in a city where there was a tiny Jewish population. In 1790 just seven Jews lived in Limerick. By 1878 a small number of Lithuanian Jews arrived fleeing persecution in their home country. Most of the Jews worked as peddlers or in retail businesses such as drapery and grocery shops. The Jews established a synagogue and cemetery. On Easter Sunday 1884 the first violent antisemitic attack and protest occurred injuring a Jewish woman and child and damaging her house. In 1892 two more families were beaten and stoned.

In 1904 the population of Limerick numbered over 38,000 souls and the number of Jews was just 170. Nevertheless, a Catholic priest, Father John Creagh claimed that Jewish peddlers and merchants were hurting the city's shopkeepers and delivered a series of damning sermons to a receptive congregation calling for a boycott of Jewish businesses. Some of Limerick's townsfolk moved one step further, attacking Jews, their homes and their shops causing serious injury and terror. Most of the Jewish families packed up and moved to other parts of Ireland as well as England and the United States. The Jerome family relocated to Bradford, Yorkshire where they became successful mill owners and cloth manufacturers. In 1970 a plaque was laid by a descendant of the family at the former Orthodox Synagogue in Shipley to commemorate his forebears who escaped persecution in Ireland, settled and succeeded in the woollen industry in Yorkshire.

Today I spin my wool with a primitive drop spindle the way that most wool is spun by individuals throughout the world. It is a slow but satisfying process and the yarn is just as good for knitting and crocheting as any spun on a home spinning wheel. I was never a good knitter, unlike my late grandmother and mother, but I took up crochet in 2017 when I was waiting for a hip replacement. My blood pressure was high and the surgeon was concerned that if it remained so he would not be able to operate. My friend and neighbour Judy suggested crochet, 'It's so relaxing. You can do it in front of the television or listening to the radio and it will keep your mind off your operation.'

Judy directed me to a wool shop in the nearby town of Kimbolton where the shopkeeper gave free crochet lessons and then sold me two hooks and some wool. It turned out to be just what I needed in the weeks leading up to my operation and it worked a treat. I concentrated on patterns and stitches and when the nurse took my blood pressure the week before the planned operation my blood pressure was fine and the operation proceeded.

Nine years ago, when our first group of sheep was shorn, we kept some of our fleeces for our own use and offered the rest free to local spinners. We advertised them on a website and met some lovely people who came to collect them. One mother and daughter arrived by car with their pet ferret on a lead! They brought it out for a walk, a sight I haven't seen before or since. They practised the ancient craft of felting. Another woman came from near Cambridge and collected a bootful of rolled fleeces to distribute amongst her spinning group. She and I became friendly and for the next few years she would come to collect wool every summer and sit and have lunch with me, al fresco, as we talked about our lives and families, plans and aspirations. Just after the Covid lockdowns she and her husband and their cat relocated to France and I hope that the three of them are fulfilling their dreams.

Most sheep need to be shorn every year before the heat of summer becomes unbearable for the animals in their woolly winter coats and to prevent the ravages of blow fly. Sadly, today in England, there is a greatly reduced market for home-produced wool and year in and year out sheep fleeces are piled up in barns or placed on compost heaps or even burned. The costs of wrapping, storing and transporting the fleeces is not compensated by the paltry price that farmers receive from its sale. Many don't bother to send it to the British Wool cooperative as the returns just aren't worth the effort involved. When we tried to give our fleeces away recently there were no takers at all. Jeremy decided to use our wool around the bases of courgette and squash plants. He had read that this kept slugs at bay whilst keeping the moisture in the soil. The experiment worked and we had a bumper crop of courgettes. Kate told us about a country programme she saw on television. The sheep farmer recommended using the fleeces around the vines in a vineyard to mulch out weeds and help the plants to grow. There is no point in wasting all the material and we will probably give this a go down in the vineyard that we planted nine years ago and which, at last, is beginning to produce grapes.

In 1950, following the decline of the wool industry the government passed a bill setting up The British Wool Marketing Board to promote the sale of British wool guaranteeing a minimum price for the product. In1972 the Shepherds Crook Mark Logo was introduced to promote and identify British wool. The logo remains a symbol of quality. Here, at The Gables, we have a long wooden shepherd's crook which I bought Jeremy for his birthday several years ago. It is by no means a twee artefact but a simple and ancient tool that has been seen in Egyptian drawings from 4,000 years ago and that some shepherds still use today. Jeremy is quite adept at using the hooked handle to catch young lambs when we want to bring them in to check on their progress, ring their tails and sometimes just to hand them to a visiting child or adult for a quick cuddle. He has yet to use the crook on a fully-grown ewe.

In 1992 the government removed the wool price guarantee and with the advent of cheaper foreign imports and man-made textiles the price of wool plunged dramatically and many farmers gave up wool production completely. Today British Wool (the more recent name for the Board) collects, cleans and sells at auction around 30 million kilos of wool each year from Britain's 32 million sheep. British Wool not only sells the wool but also encourages the use of this renowned quality product at home and abroad.

In contrast to wool, man-made fibres are causing enormous and probably irreversible damage to our rivers, seas and oceans. When synthetic materials are washed they release microplastics into the water, decimating fish stocks and adding to the millions of tonnes of plastic waste that already lines the ocean floors. Wool, by contrast, is a fully biodegradable and fully renewable material with sheep regrowing their fleeces every year. Additionally wool has fire-retardant and water-resistant properties that make it an excellent fabric for clothing and furnishings and even for house and loft insulation. Pure wool has so many excellent qualities but there are, unfortunately, some disadvantages to using the material. One year at The Gables I noticed some bare patches in the corners of our lounge. The carpet is made of pure beige wool that had been laid by the previous owner and it transpired that during the summer carpet moths had invaded and started to munch on the woollen fibres. I contacted the local pest control company who sprayed the room and explained the life cycle of the moths. Fortunately, they haven't returned but if they dare to come back I will be on the phone to pest controller Jamie in double-quick time.

When we left Devon in 1982, we weren't sure where we were going to settle. We rented a tiny two bedroom flat near Regent's Park and put all our household goods and many of our clothes into storage for 12 months. When we relocated to a permanent home in North London and unpacked our boxes we discovered that clothes moths had been feasting on the beautiful, Jacob wool jumpers that I had knitted during the Devon winters. Sadly, they were beyond repair.

When our daughter was working in Yorkshire two years ago her colleague told her about a local company making woollen socks. 'They're so much more expensive than my usual socks, Mum, but they really are worth it.' She bought several pairs for herself and for my birthday I received three pairs of stripey socks in the post. A week later I called her and agreed, 'They are the cosiest and warmest socks I've ever owned and I never want to wear any others. They are the best.' Here's hoping that home-grown British wool will regain its place in our houses, as insulation, bedding, upholstery and carpets and in our clothes cupboards and, most definitely, on our feet.

As the nights get longer and the days shorten there are several winter highlights that beckon on the horizon. The first is the Festival of Light, Chanukah, an eight-day celebration commemorating the rededication of the Second Temple in Jerusalem in 166 BCE. In 200 BCE the Land of Israel came under the control of the Seleucid King of Syria, Antiochus III who was benevolent towards the Jews and their religion. His son, Antiochus IV Epiphanes took a different approach and outlawed the Jewish religion, ordering the Jews to worship Greek Gods. In 168 BCE the soldiers of the King's army descended on Jerusalem, killed thousands of people and desecrated the holy altar in The Temple by sacrificing a pig to their God Zeus. A local Jewish priest, Matthatias and his five sons led a rebellion and in 166 BCE when his father died, Judah Maccabee (the Hammer) led a two year guerrilla war which eventually drove out the interlopers from The Temple and allowed its rededication. The legend of the Chanukah miracle is that only one container of pure oil was found in The Temple and only pure oil could be used in the golden menorah whose light had to be kept burning continuously. Miraculously the single jar of oil, enough for just one day, kept the flames burning for eight days until fresh oil could be brought to The Temple.

The festival is a relatively minor holiday in the Jewish calendar. It was instituted after the Torah had been written and there are no restrictions preventing adults or children from attending work or school.

Because one of the eight days of Chanukah often falls during the

Christmas period, in very recent times the celebration of the festival has been enlarged and become an excuse to give children presents, to hold parties and of course to eat. When our children were young we didn't want them to feel left out and we gave both of them a small gift every evening as we lit our chanukiah at home, sang the traditional songs and ate delicious doughnuts and fried potato cakes called latkes. The oily food reminds us of the miracle of the Temple oil and is an excuse to eat unhealthy, calorie-laden treats in the middle of the winter months when we are trying to keep warm. When I was at grammar school a new girl arrived from Toronto, Canada and we became friends for the year that she stayed in England. She told me that in the depths of a cold Canadian winter it was considered normal for her and her friends to pile on extra weight which gave them a layer of insulation in the snowy conditions. Come the spring they would lose the additional pounds as they ran around outdoors in the warmer climate.

Over the course of the last 50 years the English kosher bakeries have produced more and more elaborate and tasty varieties of doughnuts and it is difficult to resist buying and eating just one more. At The Gables we have to make our own Chanukah foods as there are no kosher shops nearby.

Chanukah has also become an excuse to make parties. For the last eight years we have invited our local village friends to a Chanukah get-together at The Gables. Jeremy warms plates of his home-made latkes and I hand them around to the guests. One of us makes an early morning 100 mile round trip to London to buy boxes of donuts and we lay the table with plenty of other delicacies – bridge rolls and bagels spread with Gables egg mayonnaise, mini quiches, cheese gougeres, jam tarts and strudel biscuits, fruit platters and plenty of wine, whisky and sloe gin. This year we added bottles of mead, made from Gables honey, and apple cider. Both drinks passed muster and by the end of the evening one and all left the house considerably merrier than when they had arrived. On the window sills stood the chanukiah, the candles providing light in the darkness.

The very first year, when we made a Chanukah party, Jeremy wanted to give a brief explanation of the festival to our guests. As he outlined the story Heather said, 'Yes we know all about Chanukah because we went to a party last December.' We discovered that there was another

Jewish couple who had a weekend home in the village and who had hosted a celebration of the festival the previous year. Heather gave me their email address and I contacted them and invited them over. We became firm friends. As my mother used to say to her bridge-playing buddies, 'You couldn't make it up. In a tiny village in the middle of nowhere there are other Jews. And they're not the only ones.' Although Jews are so few in number, less than 300,000 in the UK and only 15,000,000 worldwide it is extraordinary how often we find each other in the most unexpected places. We Jews have what some call Jewdar, a way of sussing out other Jews and, because we are mostly huddled together in London and Manchester with a smattering in Leeds and some of the other large conurbations, we are always excited when we find others of our tribe in out of the way places. One Christmas we were at a party in the home of friends in the village and I was talking to a young woman that I hadn't met before. I mentioned that our son had lived in Israel before he married and she said, 'I worked on a kibbutz picking oranges during my university holidays quite a few years ago.' I looked at her and then asked, 'Are you Jewish?'

'Yes, but my partner isn't and I'm not at all religious.'

We stayed standing next to each other for the rest of the evening, outsiders in arms so to speak, as she ate the mince pies on offer and drank the mulled wine whereas I could neither eat the food nor drink the wine. Wine, like food, has to be kosher and made according to Jewish dietary laws and under rabbinic supervision. The process of making wine is exactly the same for kosher or non-kosher wine but the real difference is that kosher wine must be handled by a Sabbath observant Jew from when the grapes arrive in the winery until it is bottled and even served. Fortunately for us beer, cider and most importantly whisky have, so far, escaped the requirement of rabbinic certification, although in 2013 a troubling article appeared in the newspaper, The Scotsman stating that, '..some of Scotland's best-known distilleries are bringing in rabbis to supervise whisky bottlings, which allows them to have malts certified as officially kosher.' Those Scottish distilleries with rabbinic certification can take advantage of the popularity of single malt drinking amongst observant Jews here and in America and Israel. In 2011 two enterprising young men in Connecticut founded the Jewish Whisky company which sells a range of kosher single malt whisky with rabbinic certification. These entrepreneurs are tapping into an ever-growing and lucrative market for specialist and high-end whiskies amongst the orthodox Jewish community around the world. The first Israeli whisky distillery, called Milk and Honey, began operating in Tel Aviv in 2014 with their kosher products available from 2016 and today their award winning whiskies can be purchased in over 40 countries. It seems that Jeremy and I are not the only Jews who enjoy a wee dram and I credit my late Dad with encouraging our taste for scotch. For as long as I can remember Dad kept a bottle of whisky in the drinks cupboard in our lounge and when I first started bringing my boyfriend home, on a Friday night, he would pour Jeremy and then himself large tumblers of whisky as they sat down to mull over the week. Jeremy in turn poured whisky for our daughter's boyfriend, who was not at all used to the taste when he first visited our house. Very soon he too had become a whisky snob and now it is his spirit of choice.

On a walk with the U3A, which takes place on a Friday morning in different locations throughout Bedfordshire and Cambridgeshire, I was explaining to one of my fellow walkers why I might not be able to walk on Fridays in the wintertime.

'The problem is, Frances, that I'm Jewish and I have to get back home in time to heat the food and prepare for the Sabbath one hour before sunset. It's fine in the summer time when the days are long but in the winter the Sabbath can begin as early as 3.30 pm and if we are walking a long way from Colmworth it will just be too much of a rush. It's a bit strange to understand but that's why I might not be walking next time.'

'Oh,' she said, 'I know all about being Jewish. My great grandmother was Jewish and she lived in the East End.'

I looked at Frances in shock. I knew that she and her husband and daughter had once been missionaries working abroad. I tentatively asked the next question.

'Was she your maternal or paternal grandmother?'

'Oh my maternal grandmother and I know what you're going to say. That makes me Jewish even though I'm a practising Christian.'

Jews pass their religion through the maternal line even though this wasn't always the case. In biblical times the child took the religion of the father but from the first century of the Common Era there was a shift to matrilineal descent for children born of marriages between a Jew and a gentile.

In contemporary times the status of Jew varies according to the denomination to which one belongs. Orthodox Jews will only accept orthodox conversions to the religion which requires years of study. Judaism is not a proselytising religion and the rabbis try to discourage converts so as to ensure that those embarking on the journey are really and truly committed to taking on the many obligations that surround an orthodox Jew from the moment they wake until the time they go to sleep.

The Masorti, or Conservative, movement in the UK is more open to the acceptance of converts and their conversion programme is less taxing and shorter than that of the orthodox world.

The Liberal Jewish movement accepts any child of a Jewish mother or father married to a gentile. The Reform synagogues in the UK have recently begun to accept Jewish status in a similar way on an ad hoc and synagogue by synagogue basis.

The who is a Jew question is fraught with complexities which is becoming all the more complicated with the ever-widening spectrum of Jewish practice and observance and synagogues.

Last year Jeremy and I took a series of Sunday afternoon drives to explore some of the North Bedfordshire villages. We walked for about an hour or two stopping to look at village churches and graveyards. In one churchyard I stopped by a gravestone and called Jeremy to come and look. The stone was embellished with one symbol, a Star of David, and on top of the granite were three pebbles. When Jews visit the resting place of a relative it is traditional to place a stone on the grave. There are several explanations for this custom but the two I like most are that stones or pebbles do not wilt or die, as flowers do, and the stone on a grave shows the next person who visits that there have been previous visitors to the site and the loved one has not been neglected.

I couldn't understand why a Jewish man's grave was in a Bedfordshire churchyard and the next day I telephoned the church office to speak with the vicar.

'I'm sorry to bother you but my husband and I were walking in your village and decided to look around the cemetery. On the pathway we saw the grave of a man that we assume was Jewish and wondered if you knew any more about him. I was a bit shocked not only by the Star of David but also because the man had the same surname as I did before I was married.'

'Lovely to hear from you. Actually, I'm fairly new here and I didn't know the gentleman but he was married to a lady in the village and she still comes to visit his grave. By the way,' said the vicar, 'I'm Jewish.'

'I'm sorry did you say that you are Jewish? Was your mother or your father Jewish?'

'My father but we always saw our Jewish family in Golders Green and celebrated Passover.'

I was, to say the least, surprised and wondered if the vicar's congregants knew of their cleric's origins.

'Do come and see us when you have a free Sunday.'

'That's very kind of you but Sunday is my busiest day of the week. Maybe one of these days. Thank you for the invitation.'

At the last Remembrance Sunday ceremony in the country park, after the service had ended, a tall elderly gentleman and his wife approached me.

'It was very nice to have a Jewish component to the morning and you sang the refrain beautifully.'

'Thank you.'

'As it happens,' the gentleman continued, 'My mother was Jewish but she married my father and didn't bring me up in the faith.'

'Oh. I see. According to orthodox Judaism that means that you are one of us.'

'I know but I have been brought up as a Christian and that is how I worship. However, when my mother died she was buried in the churchyard where my father and she lived down on the south coast. I felt that I ought to ask a rabbi to come and officiate alongside the vicar. After all she was Jewish. Sad to say the vicar wasn't very pleased. I just thought that it was the right thing to do for my mother.'

His wife interjected, 'And then,' she said pointing to her husband, 'He went and married me and I was born a Catholic. What a mixture. We don't live in the village but we like this church and have just started attending the services here.'

There are other instances of outing with Jews or their descendants telling me about their ancestry. My openness about our religion and the explanations as to why I can't participate in Friday night or Sabbath events allows them to tell me their secret, that they have Jewish roots in their near or distant past.

Many Jews, and I am one of them, enjoy adopting celebrity Jews. There are scores of websites informing those interested as to whether a particular famous person such as a musician, artist, actor, novelist, scientist, Nobel prize winner is Jewish or not.

The obvious standout contemporary musical figures are Bob Dylan and Leonard Cohen and the late Amy Winehouse. The lists are endless and for those who accept patrilineal descent they can claim Gwyneth Paltrow who comes from a long line of orthodox rabbis named Paltrowycz from Poland.

Perhaps this desire to gather our prominent Jews into the fold is a means of hoping that instead of reviling and persecuting us the wider world will want to recognise Jewish achievements and even embrace us. Who knows? The flip side of our achievements as a tribe is the wish to distance ourselves from those of our co-religionists whose exploits and notoriety cause us shame. Most recently Jeffrey Epstein and Harvey Weinstein and a few years before them Robert Maxwell.

As I sit in my living room, on my smallholding in the predominantly English village of Colmworth, I wonder if my neighbours know that from time to time I search the origins of so many famous British figures to discover if we share any bloodlines?

The restoration of the 300 year-old barn and courtyard in 2015 provided a perfect venue for parties. In January 2016, when our granddaughter was two years old, we held a birthday party for her in the barn. That January morning light snow began to fall and we wondered if all the children and their parents would get to The Gables. To their credit they all made the journey and the snow didn't settle. There were two unique highlights of the party. The first was the duck Jeremy brought into the barn who waddled around delighting the children and their parents. The second was the tractor ride in the trailer with parents sitting with their children as they bumped over the field at 5 miles per hours. 'Why was it so bumpy?' asked one of the fathers after he emerged somewhat shaken.

'It's a ridge and furrow field.'

'What's ridge and furrow?'

'It's a relic of ancient farming practices from the Middle Ages when oxen pulled the plough across the field and then turned around at the end and came back the other way. This created a dip in the field along the strip and next to it a high ridge of earth. There's a poem about it written by a 16th century poet and farmer called Thomas Tusser. It goes like this,

'For wheat till land
Where water doth stand
Sow pease or dredge
Below in that redge'

The fellow looked puzzled, 'What's dredge?'

'I think it was a mixture of oats and barley. The wheat needed to be planted on the drier earth and pulses and oats did better in moist conditions. This Thomas Tusser wrote a famous book called Five Hundred Pointes of Good Husbandrie and he ended his days farming an estate that he inherited not far from here in Cambridgeshire but also living for the most part in London.'

'I thought I heard you say that you wanted to turn part of the field into a cricket pitch?' said one of the other fathers who knew of Jeremy's passion for cricket.

'Well, I did until we cut the grass and realised what was underneath. There are so few ridge and furrow fields left I just don't think it would be right to flatten the land.'

When we were looking at The Gables the owner had admitted that he had never cultivated the field. As custodians of these precious five acres we are grateful for his benign neglect.

When our daughter took up a professorship at Reading University she was taking part in an interdisciplinary meeting which included academics from the prestigious and world famous Reading University School of Agriculture, Policy and Development. Her colleagues were excited to learn that her parents had a ridge and furrow field. 'They mustn't get rid of it' one of them told her.

'Don't worry they know all about it and they're determined to preserve it. You can go and visit them whenever you like.'

Two months after granddaughter's party I turned 60 and we invited friends and family from London and Manchester and the village to a daytime shindig in the barn. Daughter's friend, a kosher baker, made me a surprise birthday cake decorated with an edible photograph of me aged three. I'm a regular scribbler of birthday poems, or as Jeremy rudely puts it, doggerel. Unsure if anyone would write me a verse I wrote myself a long poem which I read out to the assembled guests. It made me laugh and cry especially as I looked out at all my loved ones who had made the trek from near and far to celebrate with me. As always, animals were one of the highlights of the day. A week before the party our ewe, Gertie, gave birth to triplets. The runt of the litter wasn't feeding and we had to bring him into the house where we could give him a bottle and keep him warm. Poor Gertie just couldn't cope with three lambs and who could blame her.

Wiggle, as we named him, needed four-hourly feeds, day and night. We felt like new parents all over again. Fortunately, lambs grow up more quickly than human babies and are less demanding. We put Wiggle in a large dog cage in the cat barn next to the party venue and halfway through the afternoon I left the celebrations to warm a bottle of lamb milk. A chorus of friends and family asked, 'Can we come with you to watch you feeding the lamb?' The group followed me to the cat barn where I sat, in my party dress, trying to get the milk into the lamb and not onto my skirt. The onlookers were enchanted.

'May I have a cuddle? Can I take him inside to show my mother?' pleaded Jeremy's cousin from Manchester. She took Wiggle into the main barn where her 94-year-old mother and her uncle, my 95-year-old father-in-law, were sitting side by side chatting and bickering away as if they were still children. Both had prodigious intellects and they enjoyed sparring with each other particularly on matters of Jewish theology. My 60th birthday party was the last time the siblings met. Their younger sister passed away a few months later, then my father-in-law and within another six months this sister had also gone to meet her maker.

Wiggle grew to be well-known locally as more of a puppy than a sheep. He would follow us around the garden and learnt to head a football and even to play on a wooden see-saw in the paddock. When he grew horns and developed teenage testosterone Wiggle became a danger to anyone entering the field. In his enthusiasm to be friendly he would run towards adults and children, bash into their legs and even push them over. He didn't know his own strength and this was only going to get worse. When Wiggle was nearly a year old, we took the difficult decision to send him to the abattoir and Chris's grandson, who had grown very fond of the lamb, was upset to find out that the sheep was no longer at The Gables. His grandpa, Chris, didn't dare tell him that he had put joints of Wiggle into his freezer and that they (including the grandson) had eaten him during a family meal. He might not know to this day.

We always found and still find the decision to cull an animal troubling. Despite being vegetarians for over 50 years we are pragmatic smallholders. One ram, bull, billy goat or cockerel will service and suffice for each group of females. Our only consolation is knowing that all the animals on the smallholding have a good life even if, for males, it is a shortened one.

Most of our chicks hatch in the warm spring and summer months. During the winter some of the birds will go 'off lay' as the daylight hours dwindle and the temperature drops. They, like us, prefer to stay inside out of the rain and cold and we notice that the egg production reduces until the days get warmer and longer. In England winter is always associated with snow, even though it doesn't snow all that often in the south of the country where we live. The song, 'White Christmas' encapsulates the childish longing which is reinforced by so many illustrations on greetings cards. When I go walking with the U3A group I often find myself singing songs with a fellow walker. Mike is an amateur crooner and performer who goes into old-age homes and clubs to entertain the senior citizens. He and I have discussed the preponderance of Jewish American composers in the lists of the Great American Songbook, not least Irving Berlin who was born in 1888 in Russia and immigrated to America at the age of five. As well as writing the song, 'White Christmas' Berlin also wrote what is regarded as the second America National Anthem, 'God Bless America.' When Burt Bacharach died Mike and I spent most of the four mile walk singing his songs and deciding which were our favourites.

On Christmas Day in Devon in 1978 Jeremy and I were decorating our cottage. It was beautifully sunny and we decided to put down our paint brushes and go for a walk. I can still remember my feeling of being left out and isolated as we passed the houses along the long country road. Inside English families were celebrating together and we were going home to paper and paint the living room. I don't think that I have ever felt more like an immigrant than on that day and the feeling of being an outsider has never left me even though I call myself English and love the country where I was born and the countryside in which I live. The feeling of impermanence and otherness is not unique to me and I know that other Jews feel that they don't quite belong. Looking back over the history of the Jewish people, one of persecution and expulsion and exclusion, it is not all that surprising that we do not always feel at home wherever we live and that, as in Germany in the 1930s, we can find the sands shifting very suddenly from under our feet.

A week after Christmas 1978 we were expecting visitors at The Old Forge. The weather had changed and snow was falling heavily. Two of our guests had already been staying for a couple of days and they resigned themselves to a few more days' holiday as the prospects of driving diminished by the hour. My old schoolfriend, Joanne and her then boyfriend telephoned us from the village phone box.

'We can't drive up the hill so we're going to leave our car here and walk through the snow. We've met a young boy in the village and he's agreed to show us the way and bring a large bag of potatoes with him.'

'Good thinking. We'll probably need more food because Trevor is here and Ray and with the two of you and us we're quite a crowd. See you later. Good luck.'

By the time they arrived the snow lay nine inches deep. I gave the village boy £2 for his trouble and the potatoes.

'Thanks very much.' He seemed pleased with the deal.

The next morning Graham and Ray, our dog Peggy and I walked back to the village to collect belongings from the abandoned car. I wrote in my diary,

'The views from the top of Stoneshill were beautiful and the hedges were covered in natural sculptures. In the evening we ate a tasty bean casserole that had cooked all day in the Rayburn alongside some frumenty that Jeremy was preparing for our breakfast. We spent a cosy New Year's Eve drinking homemade wine and watching a special edition of The Old Grey Whistle Test. On New Year's Day I walked part of the way into Sandford carrying Jo and Graham's bags as they were going to try

and drive out. In fact they later came back for dinner and one more night at the Old Forge.'

My very good friend, Marianne, with whom I trained as a physiotherapist used to say that, 'Guests are like fish, after three days they begin to smell!' How right she was. By the fourth day it was becoming claustrophobic shut up with this disparate group of friends, one of whom we had never met before and who would disappear from my school friend's life shortly after their visit.

Still stuck in the snow on the Tuesday just after New Year's Day, Jeremy discovered a sick hen in the chicken run. In those days there was no Google or internet or mobile phones. We consulted books and made whatever diagnosis we could and I was convinced that the bird had a case of Fowl Pest which was a notifiable disease. Carrying out what I considered to be my responsible civic duty I telephoned MAFF, the Ministry of Agriculture, Fisheries and Food and told them about my suspicions.

'We will try to send a vet out tomorrow. Give us your address.'

Later that day I recorded in my hand-written journal, *'....the poor little thing is in a box on the living room floor fighting for her life.'*

The next morning, Wednesday, she was dead and on Thursday morning the MAFF vet came, as I wrote, *'to inspect her and the other hens for signs of foul pest. The wind was blowing snow drifts over the road so the vet had to leave his car on top of Stoneshill. Fortunately, he thought that she had probably died of a liver condition so I breathed a sigh of relief. We sat and had a cup of tea and a chat about the EEC, livestock and such matters.'*

When I panic unnecessarily about our animals at The Gables, Jeremy laughs and reminds me of the time when I called out a vet who had to trek through deep snow because I thought that our hen had contracted Fowl Pest.

Once January has arrived the shortest day has passed, and although the weather remains cold and often icy until March, the days begin to gradually lengthen. In Bedfordshire I start to get excited, having decided that our sheep will soon begin to lamb. This drives Jeremy mad because I say it every day from the beginning of January until the first lamb is born usually four weeks later. Most sheep farmers choose to lamb when the cold months of January and February are behind them. Part of our plan, or lack of family planning, suits our Jewish calendar. If a mother ewe is unable to feed one of her lambs we will bottle feed the little one. These poddy – orphaned or rejected – lambs will need at least 12 weeks of manual feeding. If we lambed later in the year then we might still be bottle feeding as the festival of Passover approached when preparations for the festival take up a great part of late March and April. It's also fun to have new life as early in the year as possible and although the weather might be cold outside, we set up lambing pens made of straw bales in the sheep barns where we, and the new mothers and babies, can keep relatively warm. In 2018, when I was lying in hospital after my hip operation, I woke one morning to find a photograph on my iPad from Jeremy. It was the first lamb of the season. I was thrilled that she had been born but also sad because I couldn't touch or hold her and would be unable to join in with lambing that year. By Passover I had put aside my crutches, was out of pain and feeling more like my old self. Eventually with the help of a fellow physio in the village I learnt to trust my leg and was back to gardening and hauling around bales of hay, walking with both my regular groups and getting on with the day-to-day life on a smallholding. Now I just worry about how long the replacement hip will last. Jews have a preponderance to worry and I identify fully with the old Jewish joke, 'Jewish telegram – Start worrying, details to follow!' I don't suppose that my grandchildren will even understand that joke since we no longer have telegrams but I'm sure that the Jewish worrying gene will always exist.

Winter hosts one more festival which is neither biblical nor religious but more of a birthday celebration. This is Tu Bishvat, the 15th day of the Hebrew month of Shevat which usually falls at the end of January or the beginning of February and is also known as the New Year for Trees.

In the third book of the Old Testament, Leviticus, there is an injunction which forbids the eating of fruit from a tree until its fifth year. The New Year for Trees marks the birthday of all newly-planted trees. In recent times the ecological and environmental movements have used the festival to educate Jewish adults and children about the importance of nature and in the USA the date is called the Jewish Earth Day.

When our oldest grandson was still attending his religious, Jewish primary school we spoke to his class teacher and invited her to bring the pupils to The Gables for a hands-on celebration of Tu Bishvat.

'I'll have to get the permission of the headteacher, the governors and the parents but it sounds like a great idea.'

All was agreed and three weeks later, on a cold but dry day, a coach pulled up beside the gate and out trooped 30 excited children with their teacher and several parent helpers. After snacks in the barn we went outside and made our way to the apple tree corner where Jeremy had prepared six holes in the earth, assembled six varieties of apple trees, watering cans, stakes and several child-sized shovels that he had spent the previous day making from small spade heads and wooden sticks.

The children took turns in digging, planting, watering and staking the trees under Jeremy's close supervision. Once the mission was accomplished Jeremy asked them if they would, 'Come back in a few years' time and pick the apples and taste them. Is that a deal?'

'Yes!' they all shouted out. When they left their primary school the children went their separate ways and although I doubt that many of the children will return to pick the fruit I am sure that they will all remember the day they planted trees on Tu Bishvat.

Other Jewish youth groups have spent weekends at The Gables. We are not too far away from London, the kitchen is kosher and the teenagers have the opportunity to experience Shabbat surrounded by nature and animals. An annual Rabbis' Retreat is held midweek each summer which includes a group activity in the garden. One year the rabbis planted courgettes but, of course, they didn't get to eat them – we did. Chassidic visitors from the ultra-orthodox community in Stamford Hill have brought children to pet animals and run around in the field and garden. Some of these children, although born and raised in England, are more fluent in the Yiddish language of the 'old country' when their forebears lived in Eastern Europe than they are in English. In their homes Yiddish, a language based on High German from the 9th century which is fused with words from Hebrew and Aramaic and some Slavic languages, is the lingua franca and when they or their parents speak to us their English is heavily accented.

Local friends as well as those in London know that we are happy to welcome their children and grandchildren to The Gables. It is our pleasure to share this place and we know that, unless we have weekend visitors, we will have 25 hours of the Sabbath for our own private peace when we can eat, sleep, pray, read, walk and talk. At the end of the Sabbath when we light the plaited Havdalah candle, make a blessing over a cup of grape juice and smell the box of spices – the ritual that marks the separation of the Holy Day of the Sabbath from the rest of the week – we will be fully rested and ready for another busy six days on the land.

In the dark winter months we have time to make new plans and to dream of the spring. Some evenings I can idle away an hour or so leafing through the pages of the gardening catalogues that arrive in the post, tempting me with their colour photographs of fruits and vegetables, flowers and shrubs. Jeremy bases his seed orders on varieties of vegetables that have worked well in the garden in previous years. Quite often I read an article in a newspaper, or hear an item on the radio, about a particular plant that sounds interesting and we will search for seed suppliers on the internet. One of these finds has been the tromboncino, a type of courgette which develops huge trombone shaped fruits. They make delicious soups and have become a firm favourite in The Gables garden. This year my request was for a variety of red onion which supposedly only grows well in Southern Italy. It seems to be doing fine in Bedfordshire. Another unusual but delicious chartreuse green vegetable is the Romanesco broccoli whose pattern of spirals is almost too beautiful to eat. It is a natural work of art. For a few years we grew tomatillos which make excellent salsa. In spite of their name they are not tomatoes but belong to the nightshade family and are related to the orange-coloured Chinese gooseberries which we have also grown. Gardening is an adventure and so far there have been more successes than failures and as we regularly say to each other, 'We certainly eat well.'

Over the last year I have started to think about our future at The Gables. In the same way as some of our friends and family asked us ten years ago, 'How will you manage to live a Jewish life?' now others are asking, 'How long will you manage to look after all this by yourselves?'

We are realistic but we are also optimistic. When we moved we were already grandparents and entering the final third of our lives. Our age didn't stop us from taking on what turned out to be a huge challenge. We survived and thrived, made friends, raised livestock, planted trees and built a place that we are happy to share. Jeremy is still working and enjoying his latest project, the bees. I am looking ahead and thinking of ways in which we can continue to live here with the minimum of outside help. It can be done but for all of us how we live is largely a matter of luck – whether we have health and strength and whether our prayers at the New Year will be answered.

Meanwhile we will sit in our chairs, pour a glass of whisky, put another log on the wood stove and think about our next adventures hoping, as ever, for more successes than failures. L'chaim – to life!

ACKNOWLEDGEMENTS

Thank you to Tom Drake-Lee who I engaged as a writing coach when I had written many thousands of words but had no idea of a framework for the book. Tom guided me through the process of putting a book together. We had great fun during our fortnightly Zoom sessions and I was sorry when they ended. I hope that we will work together on future projects.

My dear friend Clint. You have read each chapter and made changes to the spelling (did I really study English A level?) and the grammar. I have always valued your opinion and our friendship and your input has been timely and invaluable.

My children and grandchildren (and yes that includes A – you know who you are) and my son-in-law have laughed at me, driven me mad but ultimately encouraged me to write this book. My goal now is to write more books than they have written.

My parents are no longer with us but they were the best parents, grandparents and great grandparents. They loved me and supported me in every way and they never held me back from following my dreams.

My brother, just 13 months younger than me and my confidant and friend. Scarcely a day (sometimes not even an hour) goes by when we don't talk or WhatsApp or email each other. Thank you and thank you to my sister-in-law and my niece and nephew – all of whom I love very much.

Dianne, I look forward to seeing you every Wednesday morning. You and I sit down and wait for Jeremy to make us tea and coffee and then we all have a gossip and a laugh. Your smile and humour brightens up my day and you have been as excited about this project as anyone in my family.

To all my new friends and my old friends, to my walking buddies and my U3A writing buddies and to my family everywhere in the world I thank you for your company and your messages and for reading my blog.

Rebbetzin Sara and the Rabbi, you continue to inspire me with your courage and resilience and selflessness. May the Good Lord give you strength to continue with your life-saving work. I miss you.

And to Jeremy, my partner in life's adventures, we know how lucky we are.

ABOUT THE AUTHOR

Gillian Cohen grew up in a council flat with her parents and younger brother. The family were frightened of animals and the only pet they ever owned was a goldfish that they won at Hampstead Heath Fair.

In 1974, at the age of 18, Gillian married her teenage sweetheart following a two-week engagement. She changed her name to Gill Freedman. The couple embarked on an adventure which is still continuing 49 years later.

Printed in Great Britain
by Amazon

33891487R00101